Ryan Richardson
ryan @ sbtrain . com
925-462. 3277

THIRD EDITION

f.ol # HTML and XHTML
Pocket Reference

Notepad

Dream wan
coffee cup
rrant page

nnifer Niederst Robbins

CSSZengarden

O'REILLY®

Beijing · Cambridge · Farnham · Köln · Paris · Sebastopol · Taipei · Tokyo

w3schools - com
mycelly . com
quackit

HTML and XHTML Pocket Reference, Third Edition

by Jennifer Niederst Robbins

Copyright © 2006, 2002, 2000 O'Reilly Media, Inc. All rights reserved.
Printed in the United States of America.

Published by O'Reilly Media, Inc., 1005 Gravenstein Highway North,
Sebastopol, CA 95472.

O'Reilly books may be purchased for educational, business, or sales
promotional use. Online editions are also available for most titles
(*safari.oreilly.com*). For more information, contact our corporate/
institutional sales department: (800) 998-9938 or *corporate@oreilly.com*.

Editors: Brian Sawyer and
   Steve Weiss
Production Editor:
   Matt Hutchinson

Copyeditor: Reba Libby
Proofreader: Matt Hutchinson
Cover Designer: Hanna Dyer
Interior Designer: Melanie Wang

Printing History:

January 2000:	First Edition.
January 2002:	Second Edition.
May 2006:	Third Edition.

0-596-52727-6
[C]

Contents

HTML and XHTML Pocket Reference

This pocket reference provides a concise yet thorough listing of the elements and attributes specified in the HTML 4.01 and XHTML 1.0 Recommendations. The text uses the shorthand "(X)HTML" for concepts that apply to both markup standards.

This book is organized into the following sections:

- HTML and XHTML Fundamentals
- Alphabetical List of Elements
- Character Entities
- Specifying Color

HTML and XHTML Fundamentals

HTML (HyperText Markup Language) is the markup language used to turn text documents into web pages. The fundamental purpose of HTML as a markup language is to provide a *semantic* description (the meaning) of the content and establish a document *structure* (a hierarchy of elements). It is not concerned with *presentation*, such as how the document will look in a browser. Presentation is the job of Cascading Style Sheets, which is outside the scope of this book. The current version of HTML is defined in the HTML 4.01 Recommendation.

XHTML (eXtensible HyperText Markup Language) is a reformulation of HTML 4.01 according to the stricter syntax rules of XML (eXtensible Markup Language). The elements are the same, but there are additional restrictions for document markup, as listed in the next section. XHTML includes a family of Recommendations, including XHTML 1.0, XHTML 1.1, Modularization of XHTML, XHTML Basic, and other versions still in development. This reference focuses on the XHTML 1.0 Recommendation. For details on all versions of HTML and XHTML, see the World Wide Web Consortium's HTML home page at *www.w3.org/MarkUp*.

How XHTML Differs from HTML

Because XHTML is an XML language, its syntax is more strict and differs from HTML in these key ways:

- All element and attributes must be lowercase. For example, `<a href="example.com">...</a>`.

- All elements must be terminated—that is, they must include an end tag. For example, `<p>...</p>`.

- Empty elements must be terminated as well. This is done by including a slash at the end of the tag. A space is commonly added before the slash for backward compatibility with older browsers. For example, `<hr />`, `<img />`, `<meta />`.

- All attribute values must be contained in quotation marks (either single or double). For example, `<td colspan="2">`.

- All attribute values must be explicit and may not be minimized to one word, as is permitted in HTML. For example:
  — `checked="checked"`
  — `selected="selected"`
  — `multiple="multiple"`

- Nesting restrictions are more strictly enforced. These restrictions are explicitly stated:
  — An a element cannot contain another a element.
  — The pre element cannot contain img, object, applet, big, small, sub, sup, font, or basefont.

— The form element may not contain other form elements.

— A button element cannot contain a, form, input, select, textarea, label, button, iframe, or isindex.

— The label element cannot contain other label elements.

• The special characters <, >, &, ', and " must always be represented by their character entities, including when they appear within attribute values. For example, <, >, &, ', and " (respectively).

• In HTML, the name attribute may be used for the elements a, applet, form, frame, iframe, img, and map. The name attribute and the id attribute may be used in HTML to identify document fragments. XHTML documents must use id instead of name for identifying document fragments in the aforementioned elements. In fact, the name attribute for these elements has been deprecated in the XHTML 1.0 specification.

Three Versions of (X)HTML

Both the HTML 4.01 and XHTML 1.0 Recommendations encompass three slightly different specification documents, called *Document Type Definitions* (or *DTDs*). DTDs define every element, attribute, and entity along with the rules for their use. The three versions are:

Strict DTD
> This version excludes all elements and attributes that have been *deprecated* (such as font and align) to reinforce the separation of document structure from presentation.

Transitional DTD
> The Transitional DTD includes all deprecated elements and attributes in order to be backward-compatible with the legacy behavior of most browsers. Deprecated elements and attributes are permitted but discouraged from use.

Frameset DTD

> The Frameset DTD includes the same elements as the Transitional DTD with the addition of elements for creating framed web pages (frameset, frame, and noframe). The Frameset DTD is kept separate because the structure of a framed document (where frameset replaces body) is fundamentally different from regular HTML documents.

NOTE

The XHTML 1.1 Recommendation features only one DTD that is similar to Strict in that it does not include deprecated elements and attributes.

The next section shows how DTDs are identified within (X)HTML documents.

Minimal Document Structure

This markup sample shows the minimal structure of an HTML 4.01 document. This example uses the Strict HTML DTD:

```
<!DOCTYPE HTML PUBLIC "-//W3C//DTD HTML 4.01//EN"
   "http://www.w3.org/TR/html4/strict.dtd">
<html>
  <head>
    <title>Document Title</title>
  </head>

  <body>
      Content of document...
  </body>
</html>
```

This markup sample shows the minimal structure of an XHTML 1.0 document as specified in the XHTML 1.0 Recommendation. This document is written using the XHTML Transitional DTD.

```
<!DOCTYPE html PUBLIC "-//W3C//DTD XHTML 1.0 Transitional/
/EN"
 "http://www.w3.org/TR/xhtml1/DTD/xhtml1-transitional.
dtd">
<html xmlns="http://www.w3.org/1999/xhtml" xml:lang="en"
lang="en">
  <head>
    <title>Document Title</title>
  </head>

  <body>
      Content of document...
  </body>
</html>
```

In both examples, the first line is the *Document Type Declaration* (or *DOCTYPE declaration*) that declares the DTD version used for the document. It is used to check the document for validity. Some browsers also use the inclusion of a complete DOCTYPE declaration to switch into a standards-compliant rendering mode. Note that the XHTML document uses a different DOCTYPE declaration than the HTML document and includes XML namespace and language identification in the html root element.

XHTML documents may optionally include an XML declaration before the DOCTYPE declaration, as shown in this example:

```
<?xml version="1.0" encoding="UTF-8"?>
<!DOCTYPE html PUBLIC "-//W3C//DTD XHTML 1.0 Strict//EN"
    "http://www.w3.org/TR/xhtml1/DTD/xhtml1-strict.dtd">
```

An XML declaration is not required when the character encoding is the UTF-8 default. Because XML declarations are problematic for even standards-compliant browsers as of this writing, they are generally omitted.

DOCTYPEs for Available DTDs

The <!DOCTYPE> (document type) declaration contains two methods for pointing to DTD information: one is a publicly recognized document identifier, the other is a specific URL in case the browsing device does not recognize the public identifier. The exact DOCTYPE declarations for each HTML and XHTML version are listed here:

HTML 4.01 Strict

```
<!DOCTYPE HTML PUBLIC "-//W3C//DTD HTML 4.01//EN"
  "http://www.w3.org/TR/HTML4.01/strict.dtd">
```

HTML 4.01 Transitional

```
<!DOCTYPE HTML PUBLIC "-//W3C//DTD HTML 4.01 Transitional/
/EN"
  "http://www.w3.org/TR/HTML4.01/loose.dtd">
```

HTML 4.01 Frameset

```
<!DOCTYPE HTML PUBLIC "-//W3C//DTD HTML 4.01 Frameset//EN"
  "http://www.w3.org/TR/HTML4.01/frameset.dtd">
```

XHTML 1.0 Strict

```
<!DOCTYPE html PUBLIC "-//W3C//DTD XHTML 1.0 Strict//EN"
  "http://www.w3.org/TR/xhtml1/DTD/xhtml1-strict.dtd">
```

XHTML 1.0 Transitional

```
<!DOCTYPE html PUBLIC "-//W3C//DTD XHTML 1.0 Transitional/
/EN"
  "http://www.w3.org/TR/xhtml1/DTD/xhtml1-transitional.
dtd">
```

XHTML 1.0 Frameset

```
<!DOCTYPE html PUBLIC "-//W3C//DTD XHTML 1.0 Frameset//EN"
  "http://www.w3.org/TR/xhtml1/DTD/xhtml1-frameset.dtd">
```

XHTML 1.1

```
<!DOCTYPE html PUBLIC "-//W3C//DTD XHTML 1.1//EN"
  "http://www.w3.org/TR/xhtml11/DTD/xhtml11.dtd">
```

[handwritten note: most common]

Alphabetical List of Elements

This section contains a listing of all elements and attributes in the HTML 4.01 and XHTML Recommendations, as well as a few nonstandard elements.

Readers are advised to watch for these labels on elements and attributes:

Deprecated
> Elements and attributes marked as *Deprecated* are being phased out of HTML—usually in favor of Cascading Style Sheets—and are discouraged from use. All deprecated elements and attributes have been removed from the Strict versions of HTML and XHTML.

Required
> Attributes marked as *Required* must be included in the element for the markup to be valid.

XHTML only
> Attributes marked *XHTML only* apply only to documents marked up in XHTML. Other minor differences between HTML and XHTML are noted similarly.

Nonstandard
> *Nonstandard* elements and attributes are not included in any version of the HTML or XHTML Recommendations but are well-supported by browsers.

Common Attributes and Events

A number of attributes in the HTML 4.01 and XHTML 1.0 Recommendations are shared by nearly all elements. To save space, they have been abbreviated in this reference as they are in the Recommendations. This section explains each attribute's shorthand and serves as a reference for the remainder of the element listing.

Core

When *Core* is listed under Attributes, it refers to the set of core attributes that may be applied to the majority of elements (as noted in each element listing):

id
> Assigns a unique identifying name to the element

class
> Assigns one or more classification names to the element

`style`
> Associates style information with an element

`title`
> Provides a title or advisory information about the element

Internationalization

When *Internationalization* appears in the attribute list, it means the element accepts the set of attributes used to specify language and reading direction:

`dir`
> Specifies the direction of the element (left to right or right to left).

`lang`
> Specifies the language for the element by its language code.

`xml:lang`
> *XHTML only.* Specifies language for elements in XHTML documents.

Events

When *Events* is listed for the element, it indicates that the core events used by scripting languages are applicable to the element. Additional events that are not part of the core events are listed separately:

`onclick`
> Occurs when the pointing device button is clicked over an element

`ondblclick`
> Occurs when the pointing device button is double-clicked over an element

`onkeydown`
> Occurs when a key is pressed down over an element

onkeypress
> Occurs when a key is pressed and released over an element

onkeyup
> Occurs when a key is released over an element

onmousedown
> Occurs when the pointing device button is pressed over an element

onmousemove
> Occurs when the pointing device is moved while it is over an element

onmouseout
> Occurs when the pointing device is moved away from an element

onmouseover
> Occurs when the pointing device is moved onto an element

onmouseup
> Occurs when the pointing device button is released over an element

Focus

Focus refers to the state of being highlighted and ready for user input, such as for a link or form element. When *Focus* is listed, it indicates that the following attributes and events related to bringing focus to the element are applicable:

accesskey="*character*"
> Assigns an access key (shortcut key command) to the link. Access keys are also used for form fields. The value is a single character. Users may access the element by hitting Alt-<*key*> (PC) or Ctrl-<*key*> (Mac).

onblur
> Occurs when an element loses focus either by the pointing device or by tabbing navigation.

onfocus
> Occurs when an element receives focus either by the pointing device or by tabbing navigation.

tabindex="*number*"
> Specifies the position of the current element in the tabbing order for the current document. The value must be between 0 and 32,767. It is used for tabbing through the links on a page (or fields in a form).

(X)HTML Elements

a   `<a>...</a>`

Defines an anchor within the document. An *anchor* is used to create a hyperlink to another document or Internet resource. It can also serve to label a fragment within a document (also called a named anchor), which serves as a destination anchor for linking to a specific point in a document.

Attributes
Core, Internationalization, Events, Focus

charset="*charset* "
> Specifies the character encoding of the target document.

coords="*x,y coordinates*"
> Specifies the x-,y-coordinates for a clickable area in an image map. The HTML 4.01 Recommendation proposes that client-side image maps be replaced with an object element containing the image and a set of anchor elements defining the "hot" areas (with shapes and coordinate attributes). This system has not yet been implemented by browsers.

href="*URL*"
> Specifies the URL of the destination document or web resource (such as an image, audio, PDF, or other media file).

hreflang="*language code*"
> Specifies the base language of the target document.

id="*text*"

> Gives the link a unique name (similar to the name attribute) so that it can be referenced from a link, script, or stylesheet. In XHTML, the id attribute is required for document fragments. For backward compatibility with version 4 browsers, authors use both name and id for fragments.

name="*text*"

> **HTML only**. XHTML documents use id for document fragments. Places a fragment identifier within an HTML document.

rel="*relationships*"

> Establishes one or more relationships between the current document and the target document. Common relationships include stylesheet, next, prev, copyright, index, and glossary.

rev="*relationships*"

> Specifies one or more relationships from the target back to the source (the opposite of the rel attribute).

shape="rect|circle|poly|default"

> Defines the shape of a clickable area in an image map. This is only used in the a element as part of HTML 4.01's proposal to replace client-side image maps with a combination of object and a elements. This system has not yet been implemented by browsers.

target="*text*"

> Specifies the name of the window or frame in which the target document should be displayed.

type="*media type*"

> Specifies the media or content type (MIME type) of the defined content—for example, text/html.

Examples

To a local file:

```
<a href="filename.html">...</a>
```

To an external file:

```
<a href="http://server/path/file.html">...</a>
```

To a named anchor:

```
<a href="http://server/path/file.html#fragment">...</a>
```

To a named anchor in the current file:

```
<a href="#fragment">...</a>
```

To send an email message:

```
<a href="mailto:username@domain">...</a>
```

To a file on an FTP server:

```
<a href="ftp://server/path/filename">...</a>
```

Creating a named anchor in HTML:

```
<a name="fragment">...</a>
```

Creating a named anchor in XHTML (note that some authors also include a redundant name for backward compatibility with version 4 browsers):

```
<a id="fragment">...</a>
```

abbr

<abbr>...</abbr>

Identifies the enclosed text as an abbreviation.

Attributes

Core, *Internationalization*, *Events*

```
title="text"
```
> Provides the full expression for the abbreviation. This may be useful for nonvisual browsers, speech synthesizers, translation systems, and search engines.

Example

```
<abbr title="Massachusetts">Mass.</abbr>
```

acronym

<acronym>...</acronym>

Indicates an acronym.

Attributes

Core, *Internationalization*, *Events*

```
title="text"
```
> Provides the full expression for the acronym. This may be useful for nonvisual browsers, speech synthesizers, translation systems, and search engines.

Example

```
<acronym title="World Wide Web">WWW</acronym>
```

address

Supplies the author's contact information, typically at the beginning or end of a document. It is not appropriate for all address listings.

Attributes
Core, Internationalization, Events

Example
```
<address>
Contributed by <a href=".../authors/robbins/">Jennifer
Robbins</a>,
<a href="http://www.oreilly.com/">O'Reilly Media</a>
</address>
```

applet

Deprecated. This element (first introduced in Netscape Navigator 2.0) is used to place a Java applet on the web page. The `applet` element has been deprecated in favor of the `object` element, but it is still supported and commonly used. Some applets require the use of `applet`. Furthermore, Navigator 4 and earlier and Internet Explorer 4 do not support Java applets via the `object` element. The `applet` element may contain a number of `param` elements that provide further instructions and parameters.

Attributes
Core

`align="left|right|top|middle|bottom"`
Aligns the applet and allows text to wrap around it (same as image alignment).

`alt="text"`
Provides alternate text if the applet cannot be displayed.

`archive="URLs"`
Provides a space-separated list of URLs with classes to be preloaded.

`code="class"`
Required. Specifies the class name of the code to be executed.

codebase="*URL*"
> URL from which the applet code is retrieved.

height="*number*"
> Height of the initial applet display area in pixels.

hspace="*number*"
> **Deprecated.** Specifies the number of pixels of clear space to the left and right of the applet window.

name="*text*"
> **Deprecated in XHTML 1.0.** Names the applet for reference from elsewhere on the page.

object="*text*"
> This attribute names a resource containing a serialized representation of an applet's state. Use either code or object in an applet element, but not both.

vspace="*number*"
> **Deprecated.** Specifies the number of pixels of clear space above and below the applet window.

width="*number*"
> **Required and deprecated** (because the element is deprecated). Width of the initial applet display area in pixels.

Example

```
<applet code="Wacky.class" width="300" height="400">
  <param name="Delay" value="250">
  <param name="Time" value="120">
  <param name="PlaySounds" value="YES">
</applet>
```

area   <area />

The area element is used within the map element of a client-side image map to define a specific clickable ("hot") area.

Attributes

Core, Internationalization, Events, Focus

alt="*text*"
> **Required.** Specifies a short description of the image that is displayed when the image file is not available.

coords="*values*"

> Specifies a list of comma-separated pixel coordinates that define a "hot" area of an image map.

href="*url*"

> Specifies the URL of the document or file that is accessed by clicking on the defined area.

nohref="*nohref*"

> Defines a "mouse-sensitive" area in an image map for which there is no action when the user clicks in the area.

shape="rect|circle|poly|default"

> Defines the shape of the clickable area.

target="*text*"

> Specifies the name of the window or frame in which the target document should be displayed.

Example

See map element listing.

---

b   ...

Enclosed text is rendered in bold. This is one of the few presentational elements preserved in the XHTML 1.0 Strict and XHTML 1.1 DTDs. The strong element is preferable to b because it is semantic (not presentional) and renders in bold in visual browsers by default.

Attributes

Core, Internationalization, Events

Example

We really need to leave ****right now****!

---

base   <base />

Specifies the base pathname for all relative URLs in the document. Place this element within the head of the document.

Attributes

href="*url*"

> **Required.** Specifies the URL to be used.

id="*text*"

> **XHTML only.** Assigns a unique identifying name to the element.

target="*name*"

> Defines the default target window for all links in the document. Often used to target frames.

Example

```
<head>
    <title>Sample document</title>
    <base href="/stories/" />
</head>
```

basefont

Deprecated. Specifies certain font attributes for the content that follows it. It can be used within the head element to apply to the entire document or within the body of the document to apply to the subsequent text. This element is discouraged from use in favor of stylesheets that offer much better control over fonts.

Attributes

id="*text*"

> This attribute assigns a name to an element. This name must be unique in a document.

color="*#rrggbb*" *or* "*color name*"

> ***Deprecated.*** Sets the color of the following text using hexadecimal RGB values.

face="*typeface*" *(or list of typefaces)*

> ***Deprecated.*** Sets the font for the following text.

size="*number*"

> ***Deprecated.*** Sets the base font size using the HTML size values from 1 to 7 (or relative values based on the default value of 3). Subsequent relative size settings are based on this value.

Example

```
<head>
    <basefont face="Verdana, Helvetica, sans-serif" />
</head>
```

bdo   `<bdo>...</bdo>`

Stands for "bidirectional override" and is used to indicate a selection of text that reads in the opposite direction than the surrounding text. For instance, in a left-to-right reading document, the bdo element may be used to indicate a selection of Hebrew text that reads right to left (rtl).

Attributes

Core (id, class, style, title), *Events (XHTML only)*

dir="ltr|rtl"
   Required. Indicates whether the selection should read left to right (ltr) or right to left (rtl).

lang="*language code*"
   This attribute specifies the language of the element using a language code abbreviation.

xml:lang="*text*"
   XHTML only. This is the method for specifying languages in XML documents using a language code abbreviation.

Example

```
<bdo dir="ltr">English phrase in an otherwise Arabic text.
</bdo>
```

big   `<big>...</big>`

By default, big sets the font size slightly larger than the surrounding text. This is an example of presentational HTML that should be avoided in favor of semantic markup and stylesheets for presentation.

Attributes

Core, Internationalization, Events

Example

```
Author: <big>Jennifer Robbins</big>
```

blockquote   <blockquote>...</blockquote>

Enclosed text is a quote block consisting of one or more paragraphs.

Attributes

Core, Internationalization, Events

`cite="URL"`

> Provides information about the source from which the quotation was borrowed.

Example

```
<blockquote cite="http://www.example.com">
<p>This is the beginning of a lengthy quotation (text
continues...) </p>
<p>And it is still going on and on (text continues...)
</p>
</blockquote>
```

body   <body>...</body>

The body of a document contains the document's content. Content may be presented visually (as in a graphical browser window) or aurally (by a screen reader). Although the body element markup is optional in previous versions of HTML, in XHTML it is required. All of the attributes for the body element that control the text color, link color, background color, and background images have been deprecated in favor of stylesheet controls.

Attributes

Core, Internationalization, Events; plus `onload, onunload`

`alink="#rrggbb" or "color name"`

> **Deprecated.** Sets the color of active links (the color while the mouse button is held down during a click). Color is specified in hexadecimal RGB values or by standard web color name.

background=" *URL* "

> ***Deprecated.*** Provides the location of a graphic file to be used as a tiling graphic in the background of the document.

bgcolor="*#rrggbb*" *or* "*color name*"

> ***Deprecated.*** Sets the color of the background for the document. Color is specified in hexadecimal RGB values or by standard web color name.

link="*#rrggbb*" *or* "*color name*"

> ***Deprecated.*** Sets the default color for all the links in the document. Color is specified in hexadecimal RGB values or by standard web color name.

text="*#rrggbb*" *or* "*color name*"

> ***Deprecated.*** Sets the default color for all the nonhyperlink and unstyled text in the document. Color is specified in hexadecimal RGB values or by standard web color name.

vlink="*#rrggbb*" *or* "*color name*"

> ***Deprecated.*** Sets the color of the visited links (links that have already been followed) for the document. Color is specified in hexadecimal RGB values or by standard web color name.

Example

```
<!DOCTYPE html PUBLIC "-//W3C//DTD XHTML 1.0 Transitional/
/EN"
 "http://www.w3.org/TR/xhtml1/DTD/xhtml1-transitional.
dtd">
<html xmlns="http://www.w3.org/1999/xhtml" xml:lang="en"
lang="en">
  <head>
    <title>Document Title</title>
  </head>
  <body>
    <p>Content of document...</p>
  </body>
</html>
```

---

br

Inserts a line break in the content. This is one of the few presentational elements preserved in the XHTML 1.0 Strict and XHTML 1.1 DTDs.

Attributes

Core

clear="none|left|right|all"
> **Deprecated.** Specifies where the next line should appear after the line break in relation to floated elements (such as an image that has been floated to the left or right margin). The default, none, causes the next line to start where it would normally. The value left starts the next line below any floated objects on the left margin. Similarly, right starts the next line below floated objects on the right margin. The value all starts the next line below floats on both margins.

Example

```
<p>This is a paragraph but I want <br />this text to start
on a new line in the browser.</p>
```

button   <button>...</button>

Defines a "button" that functions similarly to buttons created with the input element but allows for richer rendering possibilities. Buttons can contain content such as text and images (but not image maps).

Attributes

Core, Internationalization, Events, Focus

disabled="disabled"
> Indicates that the form button is initially nonfunctional.

name="*text*"
> **Required.** Assigns the control name for the element.

value="*text*"
> Assigns the value to the button control. The behavior of the button is determined by the type attribute.

type="submit|reset|button"
> Identifies the type of button: submit button (the default type), reset button, or custom button (used with JavaScript), respectively.

Example

```
<button type="reset" name="reset"><img src="thumbs-down.
gif" alt="thumbs-down icon" /> Try again.</button>
```

caption <caption>...</caption>

Provides a brief summary of the table's contents or purpose. The caption must immediately follow the table start tag and precede all other table elements. The width of the caption is determined by the width of the table. The caption's position as displayed in the browser can be controlled with the deprecated align attribute or by using the preferred CSS caption-side property.

Attributes

Core, Internationalization, Events

align="top|bottom|left|right"
    Deprecated. Positions the caption relative to the table. The default position is top.

Example

```
<table>
<caption>A brief description of the data in this table
</caption>
<tr>
    <td>data</td><td>data</td>
</tr>
</table>
```

center ...

Deprecated. Centers its contents horizontally in the available width of the page or the containing element. It has been deprecated in favor of stylesheets for alignment.

Attributes

Core, Internationalization, Events

Example

```
<center>
    <h1>Introduction</h1>
    <p>Once upon a time...</p>
</center>
```

cite

<cite>…</cite>

Denotes a citation—a reference to another document, especially books, magazines, articles, and so on.

Attributes

Core, *Internationalization*, *Events*

Example

```
<p>Recipe from <cite>Food & Wine Magazine</cite>
```

code

<code>…</code>

Denotes a program code sample. By default, code is rendered in the browser's specified monospace font (usually Courier).

Attributes

Core, *Internationalization*, *Events*

Example

```
<code>document.getElementById</code>
```

col

<col />

Specifies properties for a column (or group of columns) within a column group (colgroup). Columns can share attributes (such as text alignment) without being part of a formal structural grouping.

Attributes

Core, *Internationalization*, *Events*

align="left|right|center|justify|char"
 Specifies the horizontal alignment of text in a cell or cells. The default value is left. The align attribute as it applies to table cell content has not been deprecated and appears in the Tables Module of the XHTML 1.1 Recommendation.

char="*character*"
 Specifies a character along which the cell contents will be aligned when align is set to char. The default character is a

decimal point (language-appropriate). This attribute is generally not supported by current browsers.

charoff="*length*"

Specifies the offset distance to the first alignment character on each line. If a line doesn't use an alignment character, it should be horizontally shifted to end at the alignment position. This attribute is generally not supported by current browsers.

span="*number*"

Specifies the number of columns "spanned" by the col element. The default value is 1. All columns indicated in the span are formatted according to the attribute settings in col.

valign="top|middle|bottom|baseline"

Specifies the vertical alignment of text in the cells of a column. The valign attribute as it applies to table cell content has not been deprecated and appears in the Tables Module of the XHTML 1.1 Recommendation.

width="*pixels, percentage, n**"

Specifies the width of each column spanned by the col element. Width can be measured in pixels or percentages, or defined as a relative size (*). For example, 2* sets the column two times wider than the other columns; 0* sets the column width at the minimum necessary to hold the column's contents. The width attribute in the col element overrides the width settings of the containing colgroup element.

Example

See colgroup listing.

```
<table>
<col span="2" width="100" />
<col span="1" width="50" class="date" />
<thead>... (markup continues)
```

colgroup   <colgroup>...</colgroup>

Defines a conceptual group of columns that form a structural division within a table. A table may include more than one column group. The number of columns in a group is specified either by the value of the span attribute or by a tally of columns (col) within the group. Column groups may be useful in speeding table display (for example, the columns can be displayed incrementally without waiting for the entire contents of the table) and provide a system for display on nonvisual display agents such as speech- and Braille-based browsers. The colgroup element must appear before any row (tr) or rowgroup (thead, tbody, tfoot) elements with the table element.

Attributes

Same attributes as col element

Example

```
<table>
<colgroup id="employinfo">
    <col span="2" width="100" />
    <col span="1" width="50" class="date" />
</colgroup>
<thead>... (markup continues)
```

dd   `<dd>...</dd>`

Denotes the definition portion of an item within a definition list.

Attributes

Core, Internationalization, Events

Example

See dl listing.

del   `<del>...</del>`

Indicates deleted text. It may be useful for legal documents and any instance where edits need to be tracked. Its counterpart is the inserted text element (ins). Both can be used to indicate either inline or block-level elements.

Attributes

Core, Internationalization, Events

cite="*URL*"
> Can be set to point to a source document that explains why the document was changed.

```
datetime=" YYYY-MM-DDThh:mm:ssTZD "
```

Specifies the date and time the change was made. Dates and times follow the format listed above where YYYY is the four-digit year, MM is the two-digit month, DD is the day, hh is the hour (00 through 23), mm is the minute (00 through 59), and ss is the second (00 through 59). The TZD stands for Time Zone Designator, and its value can be Z (to indicate UTC, Coordinated Universal Time), an indication of the number of hours and minutes ahead of UTC (such as +03:00), or an indication of the number of hours and minutes behind UTC (such as –02:20).

This is the standard format for date and time values in HTML. For more information, see *www.w3.org/TR/1998/ NOTE-datetime-19980827*.

Example

```
Chief Executive Officer: <del title="retired">Peter Pan
</del> <ins>Pippi Longstocking</ins>
```

dfn   <dfn>...</dfn>

Indicates the defining instance of the enclosed term. It can be used to call attention to the introduction of special terms and phrases.

Attributes

Core, Internationalization, Events

Example

```
<dfn>Truecolor</dfn> uses 24 bits per pixel.
```

dir   <dir>...</dir>

Deprecated. Creates a directory list consisting of list items (li). Directory lists were originally designed to display lists of files with short names, but they have been deprecated with the recommendation that unordered lists (ul) be used instead. Most browsers render directory lists as they do unordered lists (with bullets), although some use a multicolumn format.

Attributes

Core, *Internationalization*, *Events*

```
compact="compact"
```
Deprecated. Makes the list as small as possible. Few browsers support the compact attribute.

Example

```
<dir>
    <li>index.html</li>
    <li>about.html</li>
    <li>news.html</li>
</dir>
```

div   `<div>...</div>`

Denotes a generic "division" within the document. This element is used to add a customizable block element to the document. The content within the div element is typically given a name via a class or id attribute and then formatted with stylesheets.

Attributes

Core, *Internationalization*, *Events*

```
align="center|left|right"
```
Deprecated. Aligns the text within the element to the left, right, or center of the page.

Example

```
<div id="sidebar">Content of sidebar...</div>
```

dl   `<dl>...</dl>`

Indicates a definition list, consisting of terms (dt) and definitions (dd).

Attributes

Core, *Internationalization*, *Events*

```
compact="compact"
```
Deprecated. Makes the list as small as possible. Few browsers support the compact attribute.

Example

```
<dl>
    <dt>em</dt>
    <dd>Indicates emphasized text. em elements are nearly
always rendered in italics.</dd>

    <dt>strong</dt>
    <dd>Denotes strongly emphasized text. Strong elements
are nearly always rendered in bold text.</dd>
</dl>
```

dt   `<dt>…</dt>`

Denotes the term portion of an item within a definition list.

Attributes

Core, *Internationalization*, *Events*

Example

See dl listing.

em   `<em>…</em>`

Indicates emphasized text. User agents generally render emphasized text in italics by default.

Attributes

Core, *Internationalization*, *Events*

Example

```
This is <em>exactly</em> what you've been looking for.
```

embed   `<embed>…</embed>` (or `<embed />`)

Nonstandard. Embeds an object into the web page. Embedded
objects are most often multimedia files that use plug-in tech-
nology for playback (for example, Flash movies, QuickTime
movies, and the like). In addition to the attributes listed below,
certain media types and their respective plug-ins may have proprietary attributes for controlling the playback of the file.

There is conflicting documentation regarding whether embed is a container or an empty element. Modern browsers seem to support both methods, but including the closing tag is the safest bet.

The W3C recommends the object element for embedding media objects, but embed is still commonly used for backward compatibility. If you want the browser to prompt for a missing plug-in, you might need to break conformance and use embed. Many developers use both object and embed for a single media object.

Attributes

align="left|right|top|bottom"

Controls the alignment of the media object relative to the surrounding text. The default is bottom. While top and bottom are vertical alignments, left and right position the object on the left or right margin and allow text to wrap around it.

height="*number*"

Specifies the height of the object in number of pixels. Some media types require this attribute.

hidden="yes|no"

Hides the media file or player from view when set to yes. The default is no.

name="*text*"

Specifies a name for the embedded object. This is particularly useful for referencing the object from a script.

palette="foreground|background"

Applies to the Windows platform only. A value of foreground makes the plug-in's palette the foreground palette. Conversely, a value of background makes the plug-in use the background palette; this is the default.

pluginspage="*URL*"

NN 4.0+ and MSIE 4.0+ only. Specifies the URL for information on installing the appropriate plug-in.

src="*URL*"

Required. Provides the URL to the file or object to be placed on the page.

width="*number*"

Specifies the width of the object in number of pixels. Some media types require this attribute.

Internet Explorer only

alt="*text*"

> Provides alternative text when the media object cannot be displayed (same as for the img element).

code="*filename*"

> Specifies the class name of the Java code to be executed.

codebase="*URL*"

> Specifies the base URL for the application.

units="pixels|en"

> Defines the measurement units used by height and width. The default is pixels. En units are half the point size of the body text.

Netscape Navigator only

border="*number*"

> Specifies the width of the border (in pixels) around the media object.

frameborder="yes|no"

> Turns the border on or off.

hspace="*number*"

> Used in conjunction with the align attribute, the horizontal space attribute specifies (in pixels) the amount of space to leave clear to the left and right of the media object.

pluginurl="*URL*"

> Specifies a source for installing the appropriate plug-in for the media file. Netscape recommends that you use pluginurl instead of pluginspage.

type="*media (MIME) type*"

> Specifies the MIME type of the media in order to load the appropriate plug-in. Navigator uses either the value of the type attribute or the suffix of the filename given as the source to determine which plug-in to use.

vspace="*number*"

> Used in conjunction with the align attribute, the vertical space attribute specifies (in pixels) the amount of space to leave clear above and below the media object.

Example

```
<embed src="movies/vacation.mov" width="240" height="196"
autoplay="false" pluginspage="http://www.apple.com/
quicktime/download/">
<noembed><img src="vacation.gif"> You do not seem to have
the plugin.</noembed>
</embed>
```

fieldset   <fieldset>...</fieldset>

Groups related form controls and labels. Fieldset elements are
placed within the form element. It is similar to div but is specifi-
cally for grouping fields. It was introduced to improve form
accessibility for users with alternative browsing devices.

Attributes

Core, Internationalization, Events

Example

```
<form>
<fieldset id="customer">
  <label>Full name <input type="text" name="name" />
</label>
  <label>Email Address <input type="text" name="email" />
</label>
  <label>State <input type="text" name="state" /></label>
</fieldset>
</form>
```

font   <font>...</font>

Deprecated. Used to affect the style (color, typeface, and size) of
the enclosed text. This element is no longer used in contemporary
professional web design.

Attributes

Core, Internationalization

color="#RRGGBB" *or* "*color name*"
   Deprecated. Specifies the color of the enclosed text.

face="*typeface*" (*or list of typefaces*)

> **Deprecated.** Specifies a typeface for the text. The specified typeface is used only if it is found on the user's machine. You may provide a list of fonts (separated by commas), and the browser uses the first available font in the string.

size="*value*"

> **Deprecated.** Sets the size of the type to an absolute value on a scale from 1 to 7 (3 is the default) or by using a relative value +*n* or -*n* (based on the default or basefont setting).

Example

```
<font face="sans-serif" size="+1" color="white">Obsolete.
</font>
```

form   <form>…</form>

Indicates an interactive form that contains controls for collecting user input and other page content. There can be more than one form in an HTML document, but forms cannot be nested inside one another, and it is important that they do not overlap.

Attributes

Core, Internationalization, Events; plus onsubmit, onblur, onreset

accept="*content-type-list*"

> Specifies a comma-separated list of file types (MIME types) that the server will accept and is able to process. Browsers may one day be able to filter out unacceptable files when prompting a user to upload files to the server, but this attribute is not yet widely supported.

accept-charset="*charset list*"

> Specifies the list of character encodings for input data that must be accepted by the server to process the current form. The value is a space- and/or comma-delimited list of ISO character set names. The default value is unknown. This attribute is not widely supported.

action="*URL*"

> **Required.** Specifies the URL of the application that will process the form. The default is the current URL.

enctype="*content type*"
> Specifies how the values for the form controls are encoded
> when they are submitted to the server when the method is
> post. The default is the Internet Media Type (application/x-
> www-form-urlencoded). The value multipart/form-data should
> be used in combination with the file input element.

method="get|post"
> Specifies which HTTP method will be used to submit the form
> data. With get (the default), the information is appended to
> and sent along with the URL itself.

name="*text*"
> **Deprecated in XHTML 1.0**; *use* id *instead.* Assigns a name to
> the form.

target="*name*"
> Specifies a target for the results of the form submission to
> be loaded so that results of a form can be displayed in
> another window or frame. The special target values _bottom,
> _top, _parent, and _self may be used.

Example

```
<form action="/cgi-bin/guestbook.pl" method="get">
<p>
First Name: <input type="text" name="first" /><br />
Nickname: <input type="text" name="nickname" /><br />
<input type="submit" /> <input type="reset" />
</p>
</form>
```

frame   <frame />

Defines a single frame within a frameset.

Attributes

Core

bordercolor="*#rrggbb*" *or* "*color name*"
> **Nonstandard.** Sets the color for a frame's borders (if the
> border is turned on). Support for this attribute is limited to
> Netscape 3.0+ and Internet Explorer 4.0+.

`frameborder="1|0"` *(IE 3+ and W3C Rec.)*; `"yes|no"` *(NN 3+)*

Determines whether there is a 3D separator drawn between the current frame and surrounding frames. A value of 1 turns the border on. A value of 0 turns the border off. The default value is 1 (border on). Netscape also accepts the values 1 and 0.

`longdesc="`*URL*`"`

Specifies a link to a document containing a long description of the frame and its contents. Although `longdesc` is included in the HTML 4.01 and XHTML 4.0 Recommendations, no browsers currently support it.

`marginheight="`*number*`"`

Specifies the amount of space (in pixels) between the top and bottom edges of the frame and its contents. The minimum value according to the HTML specification is 1 pixel. Setting the value to 0 to place objects flush against the edge of the frame works in some browsers but may yield inconsistent results.

`marginwidth="`*number*`"`

Specifies the amount of space (in pixels) between the left and right edges of the frame and its contents. The minimum value according to the HTML specification is 1 pixel. Setting the value to 0 to place objects flush against the edge of the frame works in some browsers but may yield inconsistent results.

`name="`*text*`"`

Deprecated in XHTML 1.0; *use* id *instead.* Assigns a name to the frame. This name may be referenced by targets within links to make the target document load within the named frame.

`noresize="noresize"`

Prevents users from resizing the frame. By default, despite specific frame size settings, users can resize a frame by clicking and dragging its borders.

`scrolling="yes|no|auto"`

Specifies whether scroll bars appear in the frame. A value of yes means scroll bars always appear; a value of no means scroll bars never appear; a value of auto (the default) means scroll bars appear automatically when the contents do not fit within the frame.

`src="URL"`

> Specifies the location of the initial HTML file to be displayed by the frame.

Example

See `frameset` listing.

frameset

Defines a collection of frames or other framesets. The `frameset` element is used in place of the body element for framed documents. The `frameset` element may not contain any content but instead defines and names some number of frames (or other framesets) arranged in rows and/or columns. Each frame is indicated with a `frame` element within the `frameset`. A frameset document contains a regular header portion (as indicated with the head element).

Attributes

Core (id, class, style, title), onload, onunload

`border="number"`

> ***Nonstandard.*** Sets frame border thickness (in pixels) between all the frames in a frameset (when the frame border is turned on). Mozilla browsers do not support `border`.

`bordercolor="#rrggbb" or "color name"`

> ***Nonstandard.*** Sets a border color for all the borders in a frameset. Mozilla and Opera browsers do not support `bordercolor`.

`cols="list of lengths"` *(number, percentage, or *)*

> Establishes the number and sizes of columns (vertical frames) in a frameset. The number of columns is determined by the number of values in the list. Size specifications can be in absolute pixel values, percentage values, or relative values (*) based on available space.

`frameborder="1|0"; "yes|no"` *(Netscape)*

> ***Nonstandard.*** Determines whether 3D separators are drawn between frames in the frameset. A value of 1 (or yes) turns the borders on; 0 (or no) turns the borders off. Netscape also

supports values of 1 and 0. The Frameset DTD does not include the `frameborder` attribute for the `frameset` element.

`rows="list of lengths"` *(number, percentage, or *)*

Establishes the number and size of rows (horizontal frames) in the frameset. The number of rows is determined by the number of values in the list. Size specifications can be in absolute pixel values, percentage values, or relative values (*) based on available space.

Example

```
<!DOCTYPE html PUBLIC "-//W3C//DTD XHTML 1.0 Frameset//EN"
    "http://www.w3.org/TR/xhtml1/DTD/xhtml1-frameset.dtd">

<html xmlns="http://www.w3.org/1999/xhtml" xml:lang="en"
lang="en">
<head>
<title>Simple Framed Document</title>
</head>

<frameset cols="200,*">
    <frame src="left.html" />
    <frame src="right.html" />
</frameset>

<noframes>
<body>
<p>Your browser does not support frames.</p>
</body>
</noframes>

</html>
```

h1, h2, h3, h4, h5, h6   `<hn>...</hn>`

Specifies a heading that briefly describes the section it introduces. There are six levels of headings, from h1 (most important) to h6 (least important). HTML syntax requires that headings appear in order (for example, an h2 should not precede an h1) for proper document structure. Doing so not only improves accessibility but aids in search engine optimization (information in higher heading levels is given more weight).

Attributes

Core, *Internationalization*, *Events*

align="center|left|right"
> **Deprecated.** Used to align the header left, right, or centered on the page. Microsoft Internet Explorer 3.0 and earlier does not support right alignment.

Example

```
<h1>Introduction</h1>
<p>In the beginning... </p>
```

head   <head>...</head>

Defines the head (also called the "header") portion of the document that contains information about the document that is not considered document content. Every head element must include a title element that provides a description of the document. The head element may also include any of these elements in any order: script, style, meta, link, object, isindex, and base. The head element merely acts as a container of these elements and does not have any content of its own.

Attributes

Internationalization

id="*text*"
> **XHTML only.** Assigns a unique identifying name to the element.

profile="*URLs*"
> Provides the location of one or more predefined metadata profiles separated by whitespace that are used to define properties and values that can be referenced by meta elements in the head of the document, rel and rev attributes, and class names. This attribute is not yet implemented by browsers.

Example

```
<!DOCTYPE html PUBLIC "-//W3C//DTD XHTML 1.0 Transitional/
/EN"
 "http://www.w3.org/TR/xhtml1/DTD/xhtml1-transitional.
dtd">
```

```
<html xmlns="http://www.w3.org/1999/xhtml" xml:lang="en"
lang="en">
  <head>
    <title>Document Title</title>
  </head>
  <body>
    <p>Content of document...</p>
  </body>
</html>
```

hr   `<hr />`

Adds a horizontal rule to the page that can be used as a divider between sections of content. This is an example of a presentational HTML element. A rule between sections of a document may be better handled using stylesheets to add a border on the top or bottom edge of a block element.

Attributes

Core (id, class, style, title), *Internationalization, Events*

align="center|left|right"
> *Deprecated.* If the rule is shorter than the width of the window, this attribute controls horizontal alignment of the rule. The default is center.

noshade="noshade"
> *Deprecated.* Displays the rule as a solid bar with no shading.

size="*number* "
> *Deprecated.* Specifies the thickness of the rule in pixels.

width="*number*" *or* "*number%*"
> *Deprecated.* Specifies the length of the rule in pixels or as a percentage of the page width. By default, rules are the full width of the browser window.

Example

```
<p>These are some deep thoughts.</p>
<hr />
<p>And this is another paragraph of deep thoughts.</p>
```

html <html>...</html>

This is the root element of HTML and XHTML documents, meaning all other elements are contained within it. The `html` element has no ancestors. The opening `<html>` tag is placed at beginning of the document, just after the document type declaration. The closing tag goes at the end of the document.

Attributes

Internationalization

`id="text"`

> **XHTML only.** Assigns a unique identifying name to the element.

`version="-//W3C//DTD HTML 4.01//EN"`

> **Deprecated in HTML 4.01.** In HTML, the value of `version` is a Formal Public Identifier (FPI) that specifies the version of HTML the document uses (the value above specifies 4.01). In HTML 4.01, the version attribute is deprecated because it is redundant with information provided in the DOCTYPE declaration. In XHTML 1.0, the value of `version` has not been defined.

`xmlns="http://www.w3.org/1999/xhtml"`

> **Required for XHTML only.** In an XHTML document, this declares the XML namespace for the document.

Example

```
<!DOCTYPE html PUBLIC "-//W3C//DTD XHTML 1.0 Transitional/
/EN"
  "http://www.w3.org/TR/xhtml1/DTD/xhtml1-transitional.
dtd">
<html xmlns="http://www.w3.org/1999/xhtml" xml:lang="en"
lang="en">
  <head>
    <title>Document Title</title>
  </head>
  <body>
    <p>Content of document...</p>
  </body>
</html>
```

i

...

Enclosed text is displayed in italic. It is discouraged from use in favor of the more semantic em (emphasized) element. This is one of the few presentational elements preserved in the XHTML 1.0 Strict and XHTML 1.1 DTDs.

Attributes

Core, Internationalization, Events

Example

```
We really need to leave <i>right now</i>!
```

iframe

<iframe>...</iframe>

Defines an inline (floating) frame within a document that is used for embedding an HTML document on a web page. An *inline* frame displays the content of an external document and may display scrolling devices if the content doesn't fit in the specified window area. Inline frames may be positioned similarly to images. The content of the iframe element displays in browsers that do not support inline frames.

Attributes

Core

align="top|middle|bottom|left|right"

> **Deprecated.** Aligns the inline frame on the page within the flow of the text. Left and right alignment allows text to flow around the inline frame.

frameborder="1|0"

> Turns on or off the display of a 3D border for the inline frame. The default is 1, which displays the border.

height="*number*"

> Specifies the height of the inline frame in pixels or as a percentage of the window size. Internet Explorer and Navigator use a default height of 150 pixels.

hspace="*number*"

> ***Nonstandard.*** Used in conjunction with left and right align-
> ment, this attribute specifies the amount of space (in pixels)
> to hold clear to the left and right of the inline frame.

longdesc="*URL*"

> Specifies a link to a document containing a long description
> of the inline frame and its contents. This addition to the
> HTML 4.01 specification may be useful for nonvisual web
> browsers.

marginheight="*number*"

> Specifies the amount of space (in pixels) between the top and
> bottom edges of the inline frame and its contents.

marginwidth="*number*"

> Specifies the amount of space (in pixels) between the left and
> right edges of the inline frame and its contents.

name="*text*"

> ***Deprecated in XHTML 1.0.*** Assigns a name to the inline
> frame to be referenced by targeted links.

scrolling="yes|no|auto"

> Specifies whether scroll bars appear in the frame. A value of
> yes means scroll bars always appear; a value of no means
> scroll bars never appear; a value of auto (the default) means
> scroll bars appear automatically when the contents do not fit
> within the frame.

src="*URL*"

> Specifies the URL of the HTML document to display initially
> in the inline frame.

vspace="*number*"

> ***Nonstandard.*** Used in conjunction with left and right align-
> ment, this attribute specifies the amount of space (in pixels)
> to hold clear above and below the inline frame.

width="*number*"

> Specifies the width of the inline frame in pixels or as a
> percentage of the window size. Internet Explorer and Navi-
> gator use a default width of 300 pixels.

Example

```
<h1>Inline (Floating) Frames</h1>
<p><iframe src="list.html" width="200" height="100"
align="left">
Your browser does not support inline frames. Read the list
<a href="list.html">here</a>.</iframe></p>
```

img

Places an image on the page. The `src` and `alt` attributes are
required. Many attributes of the `img` element have been deprecated in favor of Cascading Style Sheets for presentation and
positioning.

Attributes

Core, Internationalization, Events

`align="bottom|left|middle|right|top"`

> **Deprecated.** Specifies the alignment of an image using one of
> the following values:

Value	Resulting alignment
bottom	Aligns the bottom of the image with the text baseline. This is the default vertical alignment.
left	Aligns the image on the left margin and allows subsequent text to wrap around it.
middle	Aligns the text baseline with the middle of the image.
right	Aligns the image on the right margin and allows subsequent text to wrap around it.
top	Aligns the top of the image with the top of the tallest object on that line.

`alt="text"`

> **Required.** Provides a string of alternative text that appears
> when the image is not displayed. Internet Explorer 4.0+ and
> Netscape 6 on Windows display this text as a "tool tip" when
> the mouse rests on the image.

`border="number"`

Deprecated. Specifies the width (in pixels) of the border that surrounds a linked image.

`height="number"`

Specifies the height of the image in pixels. It is not required but is recommended to speed up the rendering of the web page.

`hspace="number"`

Deprecated. Specifies (in number of pixels) the amount of space to leave clear to the left and right of the image.

`ismap="ismap"`

Indicates that the graphic is used as the basis for a server-side *image map* (an image containing multiple hypertext links).

`longdesc="URL"`

Specifies a link to a long description of the image or an image map's contents. This may be used to make information about the image accessible to nonvisual browsers. It is supported only by Netscape 6 as of this writing.

`lowsrc="URL"`

Nonstandard. Specifies an image (usually of a smaller file size) that will download first, followed by the final image specified by the src attribute.

`name="text"`

Deprecated in XHTML 1.0; *use* id *instead.* Assigns the image element a name so it can be referred to by a script or stylesheet.

`src="URL"`

Required. Provides the location of the graphic file to be displayed.

`usemap="URL"`

Specifies the map containing coordinates and links for a *client-side image map* (an image containing multiple hypertext links).

`vspace="number"`

Deprecated. Specifies (in number of pixels) the amount of space to leave clear above and below the image.

`width="number"`

Specifies the width of the image in pixels. It is not required but is recommended to speed up the rendering of the web page.

Example

```
<p>First star <img src="star2.gif" alt="star drawing" /> I
see tonight.</p>
```

input   <input />

The input element is used to create a variety of form input
controls. The type of control is defined by the type attribute.
Following is a complete list of attributes (with descriptions) that
can be used with the input element. Not all attributes can be used
with all control types. The attributes associated with each control
type are listed below.

Attributes

Core, *Internationalization*, *Events*, *Focus*; *plus* onselect, onchange

alt="*text*"
> Specifies alternative text for an image used as a button.

accept="*MIME type*"
> Specifies a comma-separated list of content types that a server
> processing the form will handle correctly. It can be used to
> filter out nonconforming files when prompting a user to select
> files to send to the server.

accesskey="*character*"
> Assigns an *access key* (keyboard shortcut) to an element for
> quicker access.

align="bottom|left|middle|right|top"
> ***Deprecated.*** Specifies the alignment of an image.

checked="checked"
> When this attribute is added, a checkbox will be checked by
> default.

disabled="disabled"
> Disables the control for user input. It can be altered only via a
> script. Browsers may display disabled controls differently
> (grayed out, for example), which could be useful for dimming
> certain controls until required info is supplied.

ismap="ismap"
> Indicates that the graphic is used as the basis for a server-side
> image map (an image containing multiple hypertext links).
> This attribute may be used with the "image" input type only.

maxlength=*"number"*
> Specifies the maximum number of characters the user can input for this element.

name=*"text"*
> ***Required by all input types except* submit *and* reset**. Assigns a name to the control. A script program uses this name to reference the control.

readonly="readonly"
> Indicates that the form input may not be modified.

size=*"number"*
> Specifies the size of a text-entry box (measured in number of characters). Users can type entries that are longer than the space provided, causing the field to scroll to the right.

src=*"URL"*
> Provides the URL of an image used as a push button.

tabindex=*"number"*
> Specifies position in the tabbing order. Tabbing navigation allows the user to cycle through the active fields using the Tab key.

type="text|password|checkbox|radio|submit|reset|file|hidden|image|button"
> Specifies type of form control. Descriptions of each input type and their associated attributes are listed next.

usemap=*"URL"*
> Specifies the map containing coordinates and links for a client-side image map (an image containing multiple hypertext links). This attribute may be used with the "image" input type only.

value=*"text"*
> Specifies the value for this control.

\<input type="button" />

Creates a customizable "push" button. Customizable buttons have no specific behavior but can be used to trigger functions created with JavaScript controls. Data from type="button" controls is never sent with a form when a form is submitted to the server; these button controls are for use only with script programs on the browser.

```
<input type="button" value="Push Me!" />
```

Core, *Internationalization*, *Events*, *Focus*

align="left|middle|right|top|bottom" (***Deprecated***)

disabled="disabled"

name="*text*" (***Required***)

value="*text*"

<input type="checkbox" />

Creates a checkbox input element within a form. Checkboxes are like on/off switches that can be toggled by the user. Several checkboxes in a group may be selected at one time. When a form is submitted, only the "on" checkboxes submit values to the server.

```
<p>Which of the following operating systems have you
used?</p>
<input type="checkbox" name="os" value="WinXP" /> Windows
    XP
<input type="checkbox" name="os" value="Linux"
    checked="checked" /> Linux
<input type="checkbox" name="os" value="OSX"
    checked="checked" /> Macintosh OSX
<input type="checkbox" name="os" value="DOS" /> DOS
```

Core, *Internationalization*, *Events*, *Focus*

align="left|middle|right|top|bottom" (***Deprecated***)

checked="checked"

disabled="disabled"

name="*text*" (***Required***)

readonly="readonly"

value="*text*" (***Required***)

<input type="file" />

Allows users to submit external files with their form submissions by providing a browsing mechanism in the form.

```
<form enctype="multipart/form-data">
<p>Send this file with my form information:</p>
<input type="file" size="28" />
</form>
```

Core, Internationalization, Events, Focus

accept="*MIME type*"

disabled="disabled"

maxlength="*number*"

name="*text*" (***Required***)

readonly="readonly"

size="*number*"

value="*text*"

<input type="hidden" />

Creates a control that does not display in the browser. Hidden controls can be used to pass special form-processing information to the server that the user cannot see or alter.

    <input type="hidden" name="extra" value="important" **/>**

accesskey="*character*"

tabindex="*number*"

name="*text*" (***Required***)

value="*text*" (***Required***)

<input type="image" />

Allows an image to be used as a substitute for a submit button. If a type="image" button is pressed, the form is submitted.

    <input type="image" src="graphics/sendme.gif" alt="Send me" **/>**

Core, Internationalization, Events, Focus

align="top|middle|bottom"

alt="*text* "

disabled="disabled"

ismap="ismap"

name="*text*" (***Required***)

src="*URL*"

usemap="*URL*"

`<input type="password" />`

Creates a text input element (like `<input type="text">`), but the input text is rendered in a way that hides the characters, such as by displaying a string of asterisks (*) or bullets (•). Note that this does *not* encrypt the information entered and should not be considered to be a real security measure.

```
<input type="password" name="password" size="8"
maxlength="8" value="abcdefg" />
```

Core, *Internationalization*, *Events*, *Focus*

disabled="disabled"

maxlength="*number*"

name="*text*" (**Required**)

readonly="readonly"

size="*number*"

value="*text*" (**Required**)

`<input type="radio" />`

Creates a radio button that can be turned on and off. When a number of radio buttons share the same control name, only one button within the group can be "on" at one time, and all the others are "off." This makes them different from checkboxes, which allow multiple choices to be selected within a group. Only data from the "on" radio button is sent when the form is submitted.

```
<p>Which of the following operating systems have you
used?</p>
<input type="radio" name="os" value="WinXP" /> Windows XP
<input type="radio" name="os" value="Linux" /> Linux
<input type="radio" name="os" value="OSX"
    checked="checked" /> Macintosh OSX
<input type="radio" name="os" value="DOS" /> DOS
```

Core, *Internationalization*, *Events*, *Focus*

checked="checked"

disabled="disabled"

name="*text*" (**Required**)

```
readonly="readonly"
```

```
value="text" (Required)
```

<input type="reset" />

Creates a reset button that clears the contents of the elements in a form (or sets them to their default values).

```
<input type="reset" value="Start Over" />
```

Core, Internationalization, Events, Focus

```
disabled="disabled"
```

```
name="text"
```

```
value="text"
```

<input type="submit" />

Creates a submit button control; pressing the button immediately sends the information in the form to the server for processing.

```
<p>You have completed the form.</p>
<input type="submit" />
```

Core, Internationalization, Events, Focus

```
disabled="disabled"
```

```
name="text"
```

```
value="text"
```

<input type="text" />

Creates a text input element. This is the default input type, as well as the most useful and common.

```
<input type="text" name="name" size="15" maxlength="50"
value="enter your name" />
```

Core, Internationalization, Events, Focus

```
disabled="disabled"
```

```
maxlength="number"
```

```
name="text" (Required)
```

```
readonly="readonly"
```

```
size="number"
```

```
value="text "
```

ins

Indicates text that has been inserted into the document. It may be useful for legal documents and any instance in which edits need to be tracked. Its counterpart is deleted text (del). The ins element may indicate either inline or block-level elements; however, when used as an inline element (as within a p), it may not insert a block-level element because that would violate nesting rules.

Attributes

Core, Internationalization, Events

cite="*URL*"

> Can be set to point to a source document that explains why the document was changed.

datetime="*YYYY-MM-DDThh:mm:ssTZD*"

> Specifies the date and time the change was made. See del for an explanation of the date/time format.

Example

```
Chief Executive Officer: <del title="retired">Peter Pan
</del> <ins>Pippi Longstocking</ins>
```

isindex

Deprecated. Marks the document as searchable. The server on which the document is located must have a search engine that supports this searching. The browser displays a text entry field and a generic line that says, "This is a searchable index. Enter search keywords." This method is outdated; more sophisticated searches can be handled with form elements and CGI scripting.

The isindex element is not part of the form system and does not need to be contained within a form element.

Attributes

Core, Internationalization

prompt="*text*"

> Provides alternate text (not the default) to be used as a query by the user.

Example

```
<isindex prompt="Enter your search term" />
```

kbd   `<kbd>`...`</kbd>`

Stands for "keyboard" and indicates text entered by the user.

Attributes

Core, Internationalization, Events

Example

```
<p>Enter your coupon code. Example: <kbd>AX4003</kbd></p>
```

label   `<label>`...`</label>`

Used to attach information to controls. Each label element is associated with exactly one form control. The label element may contain the form control, or it may use the for attribute to identify the control by its id value.

Attributes

Core, Internationalization, Events, Focus

for="*text*"
> Explicitly associates the label with the control by matching the value of the for attribute with the value of the id attribute within the control element.

Examples

```
<label>No thanks <input name"list" value="no" /></label>

<label for="lastname">Last Name: </label>
<input type="text" id="lastname" size="32" />
```

legend   `<legend>`...`</legend>`

Assigns a caption to a fieldset (it must be contained within a fieldset element). This improves accessibility when the fieldset is rendered nonvisually.

Attributes

Core, *Internationalization*, *Events*

accesskey="*character*"
> Assigns an access key (keyboard shortcut) to an element for quicker access.

align="top|bottom|left|right"
> ***Deprecated***. Aligns the text relative to the fieldset.

Example

```
<fieldset>
  <legend>Mailing List Sign-up</legend>
  <label>Add me to your mailing list <input type="radio"
name"list" /></label>
  <label>No thanks <input name"list" value="no" /></label>
</fieldset>
```

li   `<li>...</li>`

Defines an item in a list. It is used within the ol, ul, menu (***deprecated***), and dir (***deprecated***) list elements.

Attributes

Core, *Internationalization*, *Events*

type="*format*"
> ***Deprecated***. Changes the format of the automatically generated numbers or bullets for list items.
>
> Within unordered lists (ul), the type attribute can be used to specify the bullet style (disc, circle, or square) for a particular list item.
>
> Within ordered lists (ol), the type attribute specifies the numbering style (see options under the ol listing) for a particular list item.

start="*number*"
> ***Nonstandard***. Within ordered lists, you can specify the first number in the number sequence. In the (X)HTML Recommendations, the start attribute applies to the ol element, not li.

value="*number*"
> **Deprecated.** Within ordered lists, you can specify the number of an item. Following list items increase from the specified number.

Example

```
<ol>
  <li>Preheat oven to 300.</li>
  <li>Wrap garlic in foil.</li>
  <li>Bake for 2 hours.</li>
</ol>
```

link   `<link />`

Defines the relationship between the current document and another document. Although it can signify such relationships as index, next, and previous, it is most often used to link a document to an external stylesheet.

Attributes

Core, Internationalization, Events

charset="*charset*"
> Specifies the character encoding of the target document.

href="*URL*"
> Identifies the target document.

hreflang="*language code*"
> Specifies the base language of the target document.

media="all|screen|print|handheld|projection|tty|tv|projection |braille|aural"
> Identifies the target medium for the linked document so that an alternate stylesheet can be accessed.

rel="*relationships*"
> Describes one or more relationships from the current source document to the target. Common relationship types include stylesheet, next, prev, copyright, index, and glossary.

rev="*relationships*"
> Specifies one or more relationships of the target document back to the source (the opposite of the rel attribute).

target="*name*"

> Defines the default target window for all links in the document. Often used to target frames.

type="*resource*"

> Shows the media or content type of an outside link. The value text/css indicates that the linked document is an external Cascading Style Sheet.

Example

```
<head>
<link rel="stylesheet" href="/pathname/stylesheet.css"
type="text/css" />
</head>
```

map   <map>...</map>

Specifies a client-side image map. It contains some number of area elements that establish clickable regions within the image map. The map must be named using the name attribute in HTML documents, the id attribute in XHTML documents, or both for backward-compatibility.

Attributes

Core, Internationalization, Events

id="*text*"

> **Required.** Gives the map a unique name so it can be referenced from a link, script, or stylesheet. This attribute is required in the XHTML 1.0 and 1.1 Recommendations.

name="*text*"

> **Required in HTML; deprecated in XHTML 1.0 only;** *use* id *instead.* Gives the image map a name that is then referenced within the img element.

Example

```
<map name="space" id="space">
  <area shape="rect" coords="203,23,285,106" href=http://
www.nasa.gov alt=""/>
  <area shape="circle" coords="372,64,40" href="mypage.
html" alt=""/>
</map>
```

menu   `<menu>…</menu>`

Deprecated. Indicates a menu list, which consists of list items
(li). Menus are intended to be used for a list of short choices,
such as a menu of links to other documents. It is rarely used and
has been deprecated in favor of ul.

Attributes

Core, Internationalization, Events

`compact="compact"`
> ***Deprecated.*** Makes the list as small as possible. Few browsers
> support the compact attribute.

Example

```
<menu>
  <li>About</li>
  <li>News</li>
  <li>Blog</li>
  <li>Contact</li>
</menu>
```

meta   `<meta />`

Provides additional information about the document. It should be
placed within the head of the document. It is commonly used to
identify the media type and character set for a document. It can
also provide keywords, author information, descriptions, and
other metadata.

Attributes

Internationalization (lang, xml:lang, dir)

`content="text"`
> ***Required.*** Specifies the value of the meta element property and
> is always used in conjunction with name or http-equiv.

`http-equiv="text"`
> The specified information is treated as though it were
> included in the HTTP header that the server sends ahead of
> the document. It is used in conjunction with the content
> attribute (in place of the name attribute).

id="*text*"

> **XHTML only.** Assigns a unique identifying name to the element.

name="*text*"

> Specifies a name for the meta information property.

scheme="*text*"

> Provides additional information for the interpretation of metadata.

Examples

```
<meta name="copyright" content="2006, O'Reilly Media" />
<meta http-equiv="content-type" content="text/html;
charset=UTF-8" />
<meta http-equiv="refresh" content="15" />
```

noembed   <noembed>...</noembed>

Nonstandard. The text or object in the noembed element appears when an embedded object cannot be displayed (such as when the appropriate plug-in is not available). This element is used within or after the embed element.

Attributes

None

Example

```
<embed src="movies/vacation.mov" width="240" height="196"
pluginspage="http://www.apple.com/quicktime/download/">
    <noembed><img src="vacation.gif">You do not seem to
have the plugin.</noembed>
</embed>
```

noframes   <noframes>...</noframes>

Defines content to be displayed by user agents (browsers) that cannot display frames. Browsers that do support frames ignore the content in the noframes element.

Attributes

Core, Internationalization, Events

Example

See frameset listing.

noscript

<noscript>...</noscript>

Provides alternate content when a script cannot be executed. The content of this element may be rendered if the user agent doesn't support scripting, if scripting support is turned off, or if the browser doesn't recognize the scripting language.

Attributes

Core, Internationalization, Events

Example

```
<script type="text/JavaScript">
… script here
</script>
<noscript>
The script is disabled.
</noscript>
```

object

<object>...</object>

A generic element used for embedding media (such as an image, applet, movie, audio, or even another HTML file) on a web page. The attributes required for the object element vary with the type of content it is placing. The object element may also contain a number of param elements that pass important information to the object when it displays or plays. Not all objects require additional parameters. The object and param elements work together to allow authors to specify three types of information:

- The implementation of the object—that is, the executable code that runs in order to render the object.

- The data to be rendered. The data attribute specifies the URL of the data, in most cases an external file, such as a movie or a PDF file.

- Additional settings required by the object at runtime. Some embedded media objects require additional settings that get called into play when the object plays or is rendered. The runtime settings are provided with param elements within the object.

The object element began as a proprietary element in Internet Explorer to support ActiveX and later Java applets. Browser support for the object element does not live up to the W3C's vision of object as an all-purpose object placer; for example, it is not currently possible to reliably place images with the object element. The declare, standby, and tabindex attributes were introduced in HTML 4.01 and are not supported by version 4 browsers and earlier.

Attributes

Core, Internationalization, Events

align="bottom|middle|top|left|right"
> **Deprecated.** Aligns object with respect to surrounding text. See the img element for explanations of the align values.

archive="*URLs*"
> Specifies a space-separated list of URLs for resources that are related to the object.

border="*number*"
> **Deprecated.** Sets the width of the border in pixels if the object is a link.

classid="*URL*"
> Identifies the location of an object's implementation. It is used with or in place of the data attribute. The syntax depends on the object type. Not supported by Gecko browsers.

codebase="*URL*"
> Identifies the base URL used to resolve relative URLs in the object (similar to base). By default, codebase is the base URL of the current document.

codetype="*codetype*"
> Specifies the media type of the code. It is required only if the browser cannot determine an applet's MIME type from the classid attribute or if the server does not deliver the correct MIME type when downloading the object.

data="*URL*"
> Specifies the URL of the data used for the object. The syntax depends on the object.

declare="declare"

> Declares an object but restrains the browser from down-loading and processing it. Used in conjunction with the name attribute, this facility is similar to a forward declaration in a more conventional programming language, letting you defer the download until the object actually gets used.

height="*number*"

> Specifies the height of the object in pixels.

hspace="*number*"

> **Deprecated.** Specifies the number of pixels of clear space to the left and right of the object.

name="*text*"

> Specifies the name of the object to be referenced by scripts on the page. Removed from the XHTML 1.1 Recommendation in favor of the id attribute.

standby="*message*"

> Specifies the message to display during object loading.

tabindex="*number*"

> Specifies the position of the current element in the tabbing order for the current document. The value must be between 0 and 32,767. It is used for tabbing through the links on a page (or fields in a form).

type="*type*"

> Specifies the media type for the data.

usemap="*URL*"

> Specifies the image map to use with the object.

vspace="*number*"

> **Deprecated.** Specifies the number of pixels of clear space above and below the object.

width="*number*"

> Specifies the object width in pixels.

Example

```
<object classid="clsid:6BF52A52-394A-11d3-B153-
00C04F79FAA6" height="280" width="320" codebase="http://
activex.microsoft.com/activex/controls/mplayer/en/
nsmp2inf.cab#version=6,4,7,111">
```

```
    <param name="URL" value="movies/europe.wmv" />
    <param name="autoStart" value="false" />
    <param name="UIMode" value="full" />
</object>
```

ol

<ol>...</ol>

Defines an ordered (numbered) list that consists of one or more list items (li). The user agent inserts item numbers automatically. The start and type attributes are deprecated in favor of Cascading Style Sheet controls.

Attributes

Core, Internationalization, Events

compact="compact"
> **Deprecated.** Displays the list as small as possible. Few browsers support the compact attribute.

start="*number*"
> **Deprecated.** Starts the numbering of the list at *number* instead of at 1.

type="1|A|a|I|i"
> **Deprecated.** Defines the numbering system for the list as follows:

Type value	Generated style	Sample sequence
1	Arabic numerals (default)	1, 2, 3, 4
A	Uppercase letters	A, B, C, D
a	Lowercase letters	a, b, c, d
I	Uppercase Roman numerals	I, II, III, IV
i	Lowercase Roman numerals	i, ii, iii, iv

Example

```
<ol>
  <li>Get out of bed</li>
  <li>Take a shower</li>
  <li>Walk the dog</li>
</ol>
```

optgroup

<optgroup>...</optgroup>

Defines a logical group of options elements. Browsers could use optgroup elements to display hierarchical cascading menus. An optgroup element may not contain other optgroup elements (they may not be nested).

Attributes

Core (id, class, style, title), *Internationalization*, *Events*

disabled="disabled"
   Indicates that the group of options is nonfunctional. It can be reactivated with a script.

label="text"
   Required. Specifies the label for the option group.

Example

```
<p>What are your favorite ice cream flavors?<p>
<select name="ice_cream" size="6" multiple="multiple">
<optgroup label="traditional">
   <option>Vanilla</option>
   <option>Chocolate</option>
</optgroup>
<optgroup label="specialty">
   <option>Inside-out Rocky Road</option>
   <option>Super-duper Praline Pecan Smashup</option>
</optgroup>
</select>
```

option

<option>...</option>

Defines an option within a select element (a multiple-choice menu or scrolling list). The content of the option element is the value that is sent to the form-processing application (unless an alternative value is specified using the value attribute).

Attributes

Core, Internationalization, Events

disabled="disabled"
   Indicates that the selection is initially nonfunctional. It can be reactivated with a script.

label="*text*"
> Allows the author to provide a shorter label than the content of the option. This attribute is not supported.

selected="selected"
> Makes this item selected when the form is initially displayed.

value="*text*"
> Defines a value to assign to the option item within the select control to use in place of option contents.

Example

```
<p>What are your favorite ice cream flavors?</p>
<select name="ice_cream" size="4" multiple="multiple">
    <option>Vanilla</option>
    <option>Chocolate</option>
    <option>Inside-out Rocky Road</option>
    <option>Super-duper Praline Pecan Smashup</option>
    <option>Mint Chocolate Chip</option>
    <option>Pistachio</option>
</select>
```

p   `<p>...</p>`

Denotes a paragraph. Paragraphs may contain text and inline elements, but they may not contain other block elements, including other paragraphs. Browsers are instructed to ignore multiple empty p elements.

Attributes

Core, *Internationalization*, *Events*

align="center|left|right"
> **Deprecated.** Aligns the text within the element to the left, right, or center of the page.

Example

```
<p>Paragraphs are the most rudimentary elements of a text
document. They are indicated by the p element.</p>
```

param <param /></h2>

Supplies a parameter within an applet or object element. A parameter is information required by the applet or media object at runtime.

Attributes

id="text"

> Provides a name (similar to the name attribute) so that it can be referenced from a link, script, or stylesheet. It is more versatile than name, but it is not as universally supported.

name="text"

> **Required.** Defines the name of the parameter.

type="content type"

> Specifies the media type of the resource only when the valuetype attribute is set to ref. It describes the types of values found at the referred location.

value="text"

> Defines the value of the parameter.

valuetype="data|ref|object"

> Indicates the type of value: data indicates that the parameter's value is data (default); ref indicates that the parameter's value is a URL; object indicates that the value is the URL of another object in the document.

Example

See object listing.

pre <pre>...</pre></h2>

Delimits preformatted text, meaning that lines are displayed exactly as they are typed in, honoring whitespace such as multiple character spaces and line breaks. By default, text within a pre element is displayed in a monospace font such as Courier. The example below would be rendered about the same in the browser as it appears in this book.

Attributes

Core, Internationalization, Events

width="*number*"

> ***Deprecated.*** This optional attribute determines how many characters to fit on a single line within the pre block.

xml:space="preserve"

> ***XHTML only.*** Instructs XML processors to preserve the whitespace in the element.

Example

```
<pre>
This is                 an                  example of

        text with a             lot of
                                curious
                                whitespace.

</pre>
```

---

q   <q>...</q>

Delimits a short quotation that can be included inline, such as "to be or not to be." It differs from blockquote, which is a block-level element used for longer quotations. Some browsers automatically insert quotation marks. When used with the lang (language) attribute, the browser may insert language-specific quotation marks.

Attributes

Core, Internationalization, Events

cite="*URL*"

> Designates the source document from which the quotation was taken.

Example

```
<p>In that famous speech beginning, <q>Four score and
seven years ago,</q> ... </p>
```

---

s   <s>...</s>

Deprecated. Enclosed text is displayed as strikethrough text (same as strike but introduced by later browser versions).

Attributes

Core, *Internationalization*, *Events*

Example

```
She wore the <s>ugliest</s> most interesting hat I had
ever seen.
```

samp   `<samp>...</samp>`

Delimits sample output from programs, scripts, and so on. Sample text is generally displayed in a monospace font.

Attributes

Core, *Internationalization*, *Events*

Example

```
<p>Provide alternative error messages to <samp>404 Not
Found</samp>.</p>
```

script   `<script>...</script>`

Places a script in the document (usually JavaScript for web documents). It may appear any number of times in the head or body of the document. The script may be provided in the script element or in an external file (by providing the src attribute).

Attributes

`charset="character set"`
> Indicates the character encoding of an external script document (it is not relevant to the content of the script element).

`defer="defer"`
> Indicates to the user agent that the script will not generate document content, so the user agent may continue rendering.

`id="text"`
> **XHTML only.** Assigns a unique identifying name to the element.

language="*text*"
> **Deprecated.** Provides the name of the scripting language, but since it is not standardized, it has been deprecated in favor of the type attribute.

src="*URL*"
> Provides the location of an external script.

type="*content-type*"
> **Required.** Specifies the scripting language used for the current script. This setting overrides any default script setting for the document. The value is a content type, most often text/javascript.

xml:space="preserve"
> **XHTML only.** Instructs XML processors to preserve the whitespace in the element.

Example

```
<script type="text/javascript">
  // <![CDATA[
  ... JavaScript code goes here ...
  // ]]>
</script>
```

select   <select>...</select>

Defines a multiple-choice menu or a scrolling list. It is a container for one or more option elements. This element may also contain one or more optgroup elements.

Attributes

Core, *Internationalization*, *Events*; plus onfocus, onblur, onchange

disabled="disabled"
> Indicates that the select element is initially nonfunctional. It can be reactivated with a script.

multiple="multiple"
> Allows the user to select more than one option from the list. When this attribute is absent, only single selections are allowed.

name="*text*"

> **Required.** Defines the name for select control; when the form is submitted to the form-processing application, this name is sent along with each selected option value.

size="*number*"

> Specifies the number of rows that display in the list of options. For values higher than 1, the options are displayed as a scrolling list with the specified number of options visible. When size=1 is specified, the list is displayed as a pop-up menu.
>
> The default value is 1 when multiple is *not* used. When multiple is specified, the value varies by browser (but a value of 4 is common).

tabindex="*number*"

> Specifies position in the tabbing order. Tabbing navigation allows the user to cycle through the active fields by using the Tab key.

Example

```
<p>What are your favorite ice cream flavors?</p>
<select name="ice_cream">
   <option>Vanilla</option>
   <option>Chocolate</option>
   <option>Mint Chocolate Chip</option>
   <option>Pistachio</option>
</select>
```

small   <small>…</small>

Renders the type smaller than the surrounding text.

Attributes

Core, Internationalization, Events

Example

```
<h2>Instructions <small>(Updated 6/06)</small></h2>
```

span …

Identifies a generic inline element. It can be used in conjunction with the class and/or id attributes and formatted with Cascading Style Sheets.

Attributes

Core, Internationalization, Events

Example

```
Jenny: <span class="telephone">867.5309</span>
```

strike <strike>…</strike>

Deprecated. Enclosed text is displayed as strikethrough text (crossed through with a horizontal line). It has been deprecated in favor of stylesheet controls.

Attributes

Core, Internationalization, Events

Example

```
That is a <strike>seperate</strike> separate issue.
```

strong …

Enclosed text is strongly emphasized. User agents generally render strong elements in bold.

Attributes

Core, Internationalization, Events

Example

```
Get yours <strong>while supplies last!</strong>
```

style <style>…</style>

Inserts stylesheet rules into the head of a document.

Attributes

Internationalization

id="*text*"
> **XHTML only.** Assigns a unique identifying name to the element.

media="all|aural|braille|handheld|print|projection|screen|
tty|tv"
> Specifies the intended destination medium for the style information. It may be a single keyword or a comma-separated list. The default is screen.

title="*text*"
> Gives the embedded stylesheet a title.

type="*content type*" (text/css)
> **Required.** Specifies the stylesheet language. For Cascading Style Sheets (currently the only style type option), the value is text/css.

xml:space="preserve"
> **XHTML only.** Instructs XML processors to preserve the whitespace in the element.

Example

```
<head>
<style type="text/css">
   h1 {color: #666;}
</style>
<title>Style Sheets</title>
</head>
```

sub   _{...}

Formats enclosed text as subscript.

Attributes

Core, Internationalization, Events

Example

```
<p>H<sub>2</sub>0</p>
```

sup

^{...}

Formats enclosed text as superscript.

Attributes

Core, *Internationalization*, *Events*

Example

```
<p>E=MC<sup>2</sup></p>
```

table

<table>...</table>

Indicates a table. The minimum elements for defining a table are table for establishing the table itself, tr for declaring a table row, and td for creating table cells within the row. The end tag for the table element is required, and its omission may cause the table not to render in some browsers.

Attributes

Core, *Internationalization*, *Events*

align="left|right|center"
> **Deprecated.** Aligns the table within the text flow (same as align in the img element). The default alignment is left. The center value is not universally supported.

bgcolor="#rrggbb" *or* "color name"
> **Deprecated.** Specifies a background color for the entire table. The color is specified in hexadecimal RGB values or by color name. Stylesheets are the proper way for specifying colors.

border="number"
> Specifies the width (in pixels) of the border around the table and its cells. Setting its value to 0 (zero) turns the borders off completely. The default value is 1. Adding the word border without a value results in a 1-pixel border, although this is not valid in XHTML.

cellpadding="number"
> Sets the amount of space, in number of pixels, between the cell border and its contents. The default value is 1.

cellspacing="*number*"

Sets the amount of space (in number of pixels) between table cells. The default value is 2.

frame="void|above|below|hsides|lhs|rhs|vsides|box|border"

Tells the browser where to draw borders around the table. The values are as follows:

Value	Description
void	The frame does not appear (default).
above	Top side only.
below	Bottom side only.
hsides	Top and bottom sides only.
vsides	Right and left sides only.
lhs	Left side only.
rhs	Right side only.
box	All four sides.
border	All four sides.

height="*number*" *or* "*percentage*"

Nonstandard. Specifies the minimum height of the entire table. It can be specified in a specific number of pixels or by a percentage of the parent element. Because this attribute is nonstandard, using it will cause a document not to validate.

rules="all|cols|groups|none|rows"

Tells the browser where to draw rules within the table. When the border attribute is set to a value greater than zero, rules defaults to all unless otherwise specified. This attribute was introduced by Internet Explorer 3.0 and is in the current (X)HTML Recommendations but is not universally supported. Its values are as follows:

Value	Description
all	Rules appear between all rows and columns.
cols	Rules appear between columns only.
groups	Rules appear between row groups (thead, tfoot, and tbody) and column groups.

Value	Description
none	No rules (default).
rows	Rules appear between rows only.

summary="*text*"

> Provides a summary of the table contents for use with nonvisual browsers.

width="*number*" or "*percentage*"

> Specifies the width of the entire table. It can be specified by number of pixels or by percentage of the parent element.

Example

```
<table width="70%" cellpadding="10">
<tr>
    <td>cell 1</td><td>cell 2</td>
</tr>
<tr>
    <td>cell 3</td><td>cell 4</td>
</tr>
</table>
```

tbody   <tbody>...</tbody>

Defines a row or group of rows as the "body" of the table. It must contain at least one row element (tr). "Row group" elements (tbody, thead, and tfoot) could speed table display and provide a mechanism for scrolling the body of a table independently of its head and foot. Row groups could also be useful for printing long tables for which the head information could be printed on each page. The char and charoff attributes are not supported by current commercial browsers.

Attributes

Core, Internationalization, Events

align="left|right|center|justify|char"

> Specifies the horizontal alignment of text in a cell or cells. The default value is left. The align attribute as it applies to table cell content has not been deprecated and appears in the Tables Module of the XHTML 1.1 Recommendation.

char="*character*"

> Specifies a character along which the cell contents will be aligned when align is set to char. The default character is a decimal point (language-appropriate). This attribute is generally not supported by current browsers.

charoff="*length*"

> Specifies the offset distance to the first alignment character on each line. If a line doesn't use an alignment character, it should be horizontally shifted to end at the alignment position. This attribute is generally not supported by current browsers.

valign="top|middle|bottom|baseline"

> Specifies the vertical alignment of text in the cells of a column. The valign attribute as it applies to table cell content has not been deprecated and appears in the Tables Module of the XHTML 1.1 Recommendation.

Example

```
<table>

<thead>
<tr><th>Employee</th><th>Salary</th><th>Start date</th></tr>
</thead>

<tfoot>
<tr><td colspan="3">Compiled by Buster D. Boss</td></tr>
</tfoot>

<tbody>
<tr><td>Wilma</td><td>5,000</td><td>April 6</tr>
<tr>...more data cells...</tr>
<tr>...more data cells...</tr>
</tbody>

</table>
```

td   <td>...</td>

Defines a table data cell. The end tag is not required in HTML markup but may prevent unpredictable table display, particularly if the cell contains images. The end tag is required in XHTML for the document to be valid. A table cell can contain any content, including another table.

Attributes

Core, Internationalization, Events

abbr="*text*"
> Provides an abbreviated form of the cell's content.

align="left|right|center|justify|char"
> Specifies the horizontal alignment of text in a cell or cells. The default value is left. The align attribute as it applies to table cell content has not been deprecated and appears in the Tables Module of the XHTML 1.1 Recommendation.

axis="*text*"
> Places a cell into a conceptual category, which could then be used to organize or search the table in different ways.

background="*URL*"
> **Nonstandard.** Specifies a graphic image to be used as a tile within the cell. Stylesheets should be used to position images in the background of table cells.

bgcolor="*#rrggbb*" *or* "*color name*"
> **Deprecated.** Specifies a color to be used in the table cell. A cell's background color overrides colors specified at the row or table levels.

char="*character*"
> Specifies a character along which the cell contents will be aligned when align is set to char. The default character is a decimal point (language-appropriate). This attribute is generally not supported by current browsers.

charoff="*length*"
> Specifies the offset distance to the first alignment character on each line. If a line doesn't use an alignment character, it should be horizontally shifted to end at the alignment position. This attribute is generally not supported by current browsers.

colspan="*number*"
> Specifies the number of columns the current cell should span. The default value is 1. According to the HTML 4.01 specification, the value 0 (zero) means the current cell spans all

columns from the current column to the last column in the table; in reality, however, this feature is not supported in current browsers.

headers="*id reference*"

Lists header cells (by *id*) that provide header information for the current data cell. This is intended to make tables more accessible to nonvisual browsers.

height="*pixels*" or "*percentage*"

Deprecated. Specifies the height of the cell in number of pixels or by a percentage value relative to the table height. The height specified in the first column will apply to the rest of the cells in the row. The height values need to be consistent for cells in a particular row. Pixel measurements are more reliable than percentages, which work only when the height of the table is specified in pixels.

nowrap="nowrap"

Deprecated. Disables automatic text wrapping for the current cell. Line breaks must be added with a br element or by starting a new paragraph.

rowspan="*number*"

Specifies the number of rows spanned by the current cell. The default value is 1. According to the HTML 4.01 Recommendation, the value 0 (zero) means the current cell spans all rows from the current row to the last row; in reality, however, this feature is not supported by browsers.

scope="row|col|rowgroup|colgroup"

Specifies the table cells for which the current cell provides header information. A value of col indicates that the current cell is the header for all the cells that fall below. colgroup indicates the current cell is the header for the column group that contains it. A value of row means that the current cell is the header for the cells in the rest of the row. A value of rowgroup means the current cell is the header for the containing row group. This is intended to make tables more accessible to nonvisual browsers.

valign="top|middle|bottom|baseline"

Specifies the vertical alignment of text in the cells of a column. The valign attribute as it applies to table cell content has not been deprecated and appears in the Tables Module of the XHTML 1.1 Recommendation.

width="*pixels*" or "*percentage*"
> ***Deprecated.*** Specifies the width of the cell in number of pixels or by a percentage value relative to the table width. The width specified in the first row will apply to the rest of the cells in the column, and the values need to be consistent for cells in the column.

Example

```
<table>
<tr>
    <td colspan="2">Cell 1</td>
</tr>
<tr>
    <td>Cell 3</td><td>Cell 4</td>
</tr>
</table>
```

textarea   `<textarea>`...`</textarea>`

Defines a multiline text entry control. The content of the textarea element is displayed in the text entry field when the form initially displays.

Core, Internationalization, Events, Focus, onselect, onchange

cols="*number*"
> ***Required.*** Specifies the visible width of the text entry field, measured in number of characters. Users may enter text lines that are longer than the provided width, in which case the entry scrolls to the right (or wraps if the browser provides some mechanism for doing so).

disabled="disabled"
> Disables the control for user input. It can be altered only via a script. Browsers may display disabled controls differently (grayed out, for example), which could be useful for dimming certain controls until required info is supplied.

name="*text*"
> ***Required.*** Specifies a name for the text input control. This name will be sent along with the control content to the form-processing application.

readonly="readonly"
> Indicates that the form control may not be modified.

rows="*number*"
> **Required.** Specifies the height of the text entry field in number of lines of text. If the user enters more lines than are visible, the text field scrolls down to accommodate the extra lines.

Example

```
<p>What did you dream last night?</p>
<textarea name="dream" rows="4" cols="45">Tell us your
dream in 100 words or less</textarea>
```

tfoot   <tfoot>...</tfoot>

Defines the foot of a table. It is one of the "row group" elements. A tfoot element must contain at least one row (tr). The (X)HTML Recommendations specify that the tfoot element must appear before the tbody.

Attributes

See tbody for more information and a list of supported attributes.

Example

See tbody listing.

th   <th>...</th>

Defines a table header cell. Table header cells provide important information and context to the table cells in the row or column that they precede. They are a key tool for making the information in tables accessible. In terms of markup, they function the same as table data cells (td).

Attributes

The th element accepts the same attributes as the td element. See listing under td.

Example

```
<table>
<tr><th>Planet</th><th>Distance from Earth</th></tr>
<tr><td>Venus</td><td>pretty darn far</td></tr>
```

```
<tr><td>Neptune</td><td>ridiculously far</td></tr>
</table>
```

thead

<thead>...</thead>

Defines the head of the table and should contain information about a table. It is used to duplicate headers when the full table is broken over pages, or for a static header that appears with a scrolling table body. It must contain at least one row (tr). The thead element is one of the "row group" elements.

Attributes

See tbody for more information and a list of supported attributes.

Example

See tbody listing.

title

<title>...</title>

Required. Specifies the title of the document. According to the HTML 4.01 and XHTML specifications, all documents must contain a meaningful title within the head of the document. Titles should contain only ASCII characters (letters, numbers, and basic punctuation). Special characters (such as &) should be referred to by their character entities within the title.

Titles should be clear and descriptive. The title is typically displayed in the top bar of the browser, outside the regular content window as well as in a user's bookmarks or favorites list. Search engines also rely heavily on document titles.

Attributes

Internationalization

id="*text*"
    XHTML only. Assigns a unique identifying name to the element.

Example

```
<head>
<title>The Adventures of Peto &amp; Fleck</title>
</head>
```

tr   <tr>...</tr>

Defines a row of cells within a table. A table row element contains
no content other than a collection of table cells (td). Settings
made in the tr element apply to all the cells in that row, but indi-
vidual cell settings override those made at the row level.

Attributes

Core, Internationalization, Events

align="left|right|center|justify|char"
> Specifies the horizontal alignment of text in a cell or cells. The
> default value is left. The align attribute as it applies to table
> cell content has not been deprecated and appears in the
> Tables Module of the XHTML 1.1 Recommendation.

bgcolor="#rrggbb" *or* "color name"
> **Deprecated.** Specifies a color to be used in the row. A row's
> background color overrides the color specified at the table
> level.

char="character"
> Specifies a character along which the cell contents will be
> aligned when align is set to char. The default character is a
> decimal point (language-appropriate). This attribute is gener-
> ally not supported by current browsers.

charoff="length"
> Specifies the offset distance to the first alignment character on
> each line. If a line doesn't use an alignment character, it
> should be horizontally shifted to end at the alignment posi-
> tion. This attribute is generally not supported by current
> browsers.

valign="top|middle|bottom|baseline"
> Specifies the vertical alignment of text in the cells of a
> column. The valign attribute as it applies to table cell content
> has not been deprecated and appears in the Tables Module of
> the XHTML 1.1 Recommendation.

Example

```
<table>
<tr>
    <td>cell 1</td><td>cell 2</td>
</tr>
```

```
<tr>
     <td>cell 3</td><td>cell 4</td>
</tr>
</table>
```

tt

Formats enclosed text as teletype text. The text enclosed in the tt element is generally displayed in a monospace font such as Courier.

Attributes

Core, Internationalization, Events

Example

```
<p>Enter your birthday (Ex: <tt>07.19.1975</tt>):</p>
```

u

Deprecated. Enclosed text is underlined when displayed. Underlined text may be confused as a hypertext link, but if underlining is required, Cascading Style Sheets is the preferred method.

Attributes

Core, Internationalization, Events

Example

```
<p><u>Underlined text</u> may be mistaken for a link.</p>
```

ul

Defines an unordered list, in which list items (li) have no sequence. By default, browsers insert bullets before each item in an unordered list. Lists may be formatted in any fashion (including as horizontal navigation elements) using Cascading Style Sheet properties.

Attributes

Core, Internationalization, Events

compact="compact"
> **Deprecated.** Displays the list block as small as possible. Few browsers support this attribute.

type="disc|circle|square"
> **Deprecated.** Defines the shape of the bullets used for each list item.

Example

```
<ul>
    <li>About</li>
    <li>Portfolio</li>
    <li>Blog</li>
    <li>Contact</li>
</ul>
```

var   <var>...</var>

Indicates an instance of a variable or program argument, usually rendered in italics.

Attributes

Core, Internationalization, Events

Example

```
<var>myString</var> = 'hello world';
```

Character Entities

Characters not found in the normal alphanumeric character set, such as < and &, must be specified in HTML and XHTML documents using character references. This process is known as *escaping* the character. In (X)HTML documents, escaped characters are indicated by character references that begin with & and end with ;. The character may be referred to by its Numeric Character Reference (NCR) or a predefined character entity name.

A Numeric Character Reference refers to a character by its Unicode code point in either decimal or hexadecimal form.

Decimal character references use the syntax &#nnnn;. Hexadecimal values are indicated by an "x": &#xhhhh;. For example, the less-than (<) character could be identified as < (decimal) or &#x3C (hexadecimal).

Character entities are abbreviated names for characters, such as < for the less-than symbol. Character entities are predefined in the DTDs of markup languages such as HTML and XHMTL as a convenience to authors because they may be easier to remember than Numeric Character References.

ASCII Character Set

HTML and XHTML documents use the standard 7-bit ASCII character set in their source. The first 31 characters in ASCII (not listed) are such device controls as backspace (&#08;) and carriage return () and are not appropriate for use in HTML documents.

HTML 4.01 defines only four entities in this character range—less than (<, <), greater than (<, >), ampersand (&, &), and quotation mark (", ")—that are necessary for escaping characters that may be interpreted as markup. XHTML also includes the ' entity that is included in every XML language. In XHTML documents, the ampersand symbol (&) must always be escaped in attribute values. For better compatibility with XML parsers, authors should use numerical character references instead of named character references for all other character entities.

Numeric character entities may also be represented by their hexadecimal equivalents. Hexadecimal values are preceded by an x. For example, the hexadecimal character reference for the less-than symbol is written <.

Decimal	Entity	Symbol	Description
 			Space
!		!	Exclamation point

Decimal	Entity	Symbol	Description
"	"	"	Quotation mark
#		#	Octothorpe
$		$	Dollar symbol
%		%	Percent symbol
&	&	&	Ampersand
'	' **(XML/XHTML only)**	'	Apostrophe (single quote)
(		(	Left parenthesis
)		)	Right parenthesis
*		*	Asterisk
+		+	Plus sign
,		,	Comma
-		-	Hyphen
.		.	Period
/		/	Slash
0–9		0–9	Digits 0–9
:		:	Colon
;		;	Semicolon
<	<	<	Less than
=		=	Equals sign
>	>	>	Greater than
?		?	Question mark
@		@	Commercial at sign
A–Z		A–Z	Letters A–Z
[		[	Left square bracket
\		\	Backslash
]		]	Right square bracket
^		^	Caret

Decimal	Entity	Symbol	Description
_		_	Underscore
`		`	Grave accent (no letter)
a– z		a–z	Letters a–z
{		{	Left curly brace
|				Vertical bar
}		}	Right curly brace
~		~	Tilde

Nonstandard Entities (‚–Ÿ)

The character references numbered 130 through 159 are not defined in HTML and therefore are invalid characters that should be avoided.

Some nonstandard numerical entities in this range are supported by browsers (such as &151; for an em dash); however, they all have standard equivalents (listed in the "General Punctuation" section). If you need an em dash, use &8212; or — instead.

Latin-1 (ISO-8859-1)

Decimal	Entity	Symbol	Description
			Nonbreaking space
¡	¡	¡	Inverted exclamation mark
¢	¢	¢	Cent sign
£	£	£	Pound symbol
¤	¤	¤	General currency symbol
¥	¥	¥	Yen symbol
¦	¦	¦	Broken vertical bar
§	§	§	Section sign

Decimal	Entity	Symbol	Description
¨	¨	¨	Umlaut
©	©	©	Copyright
ª	ª	a	Feminine ordinal
«	«	«	Left angle quote
¬	¬	¬	Not sign
­	­	–	Soft hyphen
®	®	®	Registered trademark
¯	¯	¯	Macron accent
°	°	°	Degree sign
±	±	±	Plus or minus
²	²	2	Superscript 2
³	³	3	Superscript 3
´	´	´	Acute accent (no letter)
µ	µ	μ	Micron (Greek mu)
¶	¶	¶	Paragraph sign
·	·	·	Middle dot
¸	¸	¸	Cedilla
¹	¹	1	Superscript 1
º	º	o	Masculine ordinal
»	»	»	Right angle quote
¼	¼	1/4	Fraction one-fourth
½	½	1/2	Fraction one-half
¾	¾	3/4	Fraction three-fourths
¿	¿	¿	Inverted question mark
À	À	À	Capital A, grave accent

Decimal	Entity	Symbol	Description
&#193;	&Aacute;	Á	Capital A, acute accent
&#194;	&Acirc;	Â	Capital A, circumflex accent
&#195;	&Atilde;	Ã	Capital A, tilde accent
&#196;	&Auml;	Ä	Capital A, umlaut
&#197;	&Aring	Å	Capital A, ring
&#198;	&AElig;	Æ	Capital AE ligature
&#199;	&Ccedil;	Ç	Capital C, cedilla
&#200;	&Egrave	È	Capital E, grave accent
&#201;	&Eacute;	É	Capital E, acute accent
&#202;	&Ecirc;	Ê	Capital E, circumflex accent
&#203;	&Euml;	Ë	Capital E, umlaut
&#204;	&Igrave;	Ì	Capital I, grave accent
&#205;	&Iacute;	Í	Capital I, acute accent
&#206;	&Icirc;	Î	Capital I, circumflex accent
&#207;	&Iuml;	Ï	Capital I, umlaut
&#208;	&ETH;	Ð	Capital eth, Icelandic
&#209;	&Ntilde;	Ñ	Capital N, tilde
&#210;	&Ograve;	Ò	Capital O, grave accent
&#211;	&Oacute;	Ó	Capital O, acute accent
&#212;	&Ocirc;	Ô	Capital O, circumflex accent

Decimal	Entity	Symbol	Description
&#213;	&Otilde;	Õ	Capital O, tilde accent
&#214;	&Ouml;	Ö	Capital O, umlaut
&#215;	&times;	×	Multiplication sign
&#216;	&Oslash;	Ø	Capital O, slash
&#217;	&Ugrave;	Ù	Capital U, grave accent
&#218;	&Uacute;	Ú	Capital U, acute accent
&#219;	&Ucirc;	Û	Capital U, circumflex accent
&#220;	&Uuml;	Ü	Capital U, umlaut
&#221;	&Yacute;	Ý	Capital Y, acute accent
&#222;	&THORN;	Þ	Capital Thorn, Icelandic
&#223;	&szlig;	ß	Small sz ligature, German
&#224;	&agrave;	à	Small a, grave accent
&#225;	&aacute;	á	Small a, acute accent
&#226;	&acirc;	â	Small a, circumflex accent
&#227;	&atilde;	ã	Small a, tilde
&#228;	&auml;	ä	Small a, umlaut
&#229;	&aring;	å	Small a, ring
&#230;	&aelig;	æ	Small ae ligature
&#231;	&ccedil;	ç	Small c, cedilla
&#232;	&egrave;	è	Small e, grave accent
&#233;	&eacute;	é	Small e, acute accent

Decimal	Entity	Symbol	Description
ê	ê	ê	Small e, circumflex accent
ë	ë	ë	Small e, umlaut
ì	ì	ì	Small i, grave accent
í	í	í	Small i, acute accent
î	î	î	Small i, circumflex accent
ï	ï	ï	Small i, umlaut
ð	ð	∂	Small eth, Icelandic
ñ	ñ	ñ	Small n, tilde
ò	ò	ò	Small o, grave accent
ó	ó	ó	Small o, acute accent
ô	ô	ô	Small o, circumflex accent
õ	õ	õ	Small o, tilde
ö	ö	ö	Small o, umlaut
÷	÷	÷	Division sign
ø	ø	ø	Small o, slash
ù	ù	ù	Small u, grave accent
ú	ú	ú	Small u, acute accent
û	û	û	Small u, circumflex accent
ü	ü	ü	Small u, umlaut
ý	ý	ý	Small y, acute accent
þ	þ	þ	Small thorn, Icelandic
ÿ	ÿ	ÿ	Small y, umlaut

Latin Extended-A

Decimal	Entity	Symbol	Description
Œ	Œ	Œ	Capital ligature OE
œ	œ	œ	Small ligature oe
Š	Š	Š	Capital S, caron
š	š	š	Small s, caron
&#376	Ÿ	Ÿ	Capital Y, umlaut

Latin Extended-B

Decimal	Entity	Symbol	Description
ƒ	ƒ	ƒ	Small f with hook

Spacing Modifier Letters

Decimal	Entity	Symbol	Description
ˆ	ˆ	ˆ	Circumflex accent
˜	˜	˜	Tilde

Greek

Decimal	Entity	Symbol	Description
Α	Α	Α	Greek capital alpha
Β	Β	Β	Greek capital beta
Γ	Γ	Γ	Greek capital gamma
Δ	Δ	Δ	Greek capital delta
Ε	Ε	E	Greek capital epsilon
Ζ	Ζ	Z	Greek capital zeta
&#919	Η	H	Greek capital eta

Decimal	Entity	Symbol	Description
Θ	Θ	Θ	Greek capital theta
Ι	Ι	I	Greek capital iota
Κ	Κ	K	Greek capital kappa
Λ	Λ	Λ	Greek capital lambda
Μ	Μ	M	Greek capital mu
Ν	Ν	N	Greek capital nu
Ξ	Ξ	Ξ	Greek capital xi
Ο	Ο	O	Greek capital omicron
Π	Π	π	Greek capital pi
Ρ	Ρ	P	Greek capital rho
Σ	Σ	Σ	Greek captial sigma
Τ	Τ	T	Greek capital tau
Υ	Υ	Y	Greek capital upsilon
Φ	Φ	Φ	Greek capital phi
Χ	Χ	X	Greek capital chi
Ψ	Ψ	Ψ	Greek capital psi
Ω	Ω	Ω	Greek capital omega
α	α	α	Greek small alpha
β	β	β	Greek small beta
γ	γ	γ	Greek small gamma
δ	δ	δ	Greek small delta
ε	ε	ε	Greek small epsilon
ζ	ζ	ζ	Greek small zeta
η	η	η	Greek small eta
θ	θ	θ	Greek small theta

Decimal	Entity	Symbol	Description
ι	ι	ι	Greek small iota
κ	κ	κ	Greek small kappa
λ	λ	λ	Greek small lambda
μ	μ	μ	Greek small mu
ν	ν	ν	Greek small nu
ξ	ξ	ξ	Greek small xi
ο	ο	o	Greek small omicron
π	π	π	Greek small pi
ρ	ρ	ρ	Greek small rho
ς	ς	ς	Greek small letter final sigma
σ	σ	σ	Greek small sigma
τ	τ	τ	Greek small tau
υ	υ	υ	Greek small upsilon
φ	φ	φ	Greek small phi
χ	χ	χ	Greek small chi
ψ	ψ	ψ	Greek small psi
ω	ω	ω	Greek small omega
ϑ	ϑ	ϑ	Greek small theta symbol
ϒ	ϒ	ϒ	Greek upsilon with hook
ϖ	ϖ	ϖ	Greek pi symbol

General Punctuation

Decimal	Entity	Symbol	Description
			En space
			Em space
			Thin space

Decimal	Entity	Symbol	Description
‌	‌	Nonprinting	Zero-width nonjoiner
‍	‍	Nonprinting	Zero-width joiner
‎	‎	Nonprinting	Left-to-right mark
&#8207	‏	Nonprinting	Right-to-left mark
–	–	–	Endash
—	—	—	Emdash
‘	‘	`	Left single quotation mark
’	’	'	Right single quotation mark
‚	‚	‚	Single low-9 quotation mark
“	“	"	Left double quotation mark
”	”	"	Right double quotation mark
„	„	„	Double low-9 quotation mark
†	†	†	Dagger
‡	‡	‡	Double dagger
•	•	•	Bullet
…	&hellep;	…	Ellipses
‰	‰	‰	Per mille symbol (per thousand)
′	′	'	Prime, minutes, feet
″	″	"	Double prime, seconds, inches
‹	‹	'	Single left angle quotation (**nonstandard**)

Decimal	Entity	Symbol	Description
›	›	›	Single right angle quotation (**nonstandard**)
‾	‾	‾	Overline
⁄	⁄	/	Fraction slash
€	€	€	Euro symbol

Letter-like Symbols

Decimal	Entity	Symbol	Description
ℑ	ℑ	ℑ	Blackletter capital I, imaginary part
℘	℘	℘	Script capital P, power set
ℜ	ℜ	ℜ	Blackletter capital R, real part
™	™	™	Trademark sign
ℵ	ℵ	ℵ	Alef symbol, or first transfinite cardinal

Arrows

Decimal	Entity	Symbol	Description
←	←	←	Left arrow
↑	↑	↑	Up arrow
→	→	→	Right arrow
↓	↓	↓	Down arrow
↔	↔	↔	Left-right arrow
↵	↵	↵	Down arrow with corner leftward
⇐	⇐	⇐	Leftward double arrow

Decimal	Entity	Symbol	Description
⇑	⇑	⇑	Upward double arrow
⇒	⇒	⇒	Rightward double arrow
⇓	⇓	⇓	Downward double arrow
⇔	⇔	⇔	Left-right double arrow

Mathematical Operators

Decimal	Entity	Symbol	Description
∀	∀	∀	For all
∂	∂	∂	Partial differential
∃	∃	∃	There exists
∅	∅	∅	Empty set, null set, diameter
∇	∇	∇	Nabla, backward difference
∈	∈	∈	Element of
&#8713	∉	∉	Not an element of
∋	∋	∋	Contains as a member
∏	∏	∏	N-ary product, product sign
∑	∑	∑	N-ary summation
−	−	−	Minus sign
∗	∗	*	Asterisk operator
√	√	√	Square root, radical sign
∝	∝	∝	Proportional
∞	∞	∞	Infinity symbol
∠	∠	∠	Angle

Decimal	Entity	Symbol	Description
∧	∧	∧	Logical and, wedge
∨	∨	∨	Logical or, vee
∩	∩	∩	Intersection, cap
∪	∪	∪	Union, cup
∫	∫	∫	Integral
∴	∴	∴	Therefore
∼	∼	~	Tilde operator, varies with, similar to
≅	≅	≅	Approximately equal to
≈	≈	≈	Almost equal to, asymptotic to
≠	≠	≠	Not equal to
≡	≡	≡	Identical to
≤	≤	≤	Less than or equal to
≥	≥	≥	Greater than or equal to
⊂	⊂	⊂	Subset of
⊃	⊃	⊃	Superset of
⊄	⊄	⊄	Not a subset of
⊆	&sube	⊆	Subset of or equal to
⊇	&supe	⊇	Superset of or equal to
⊕	⊕	⊕	Circled plus, direct sum
⊗	⊗	⊗	Circled times, vector product
⊥	⊥	⊥	Up tack, orthogonal to, perpendicular
⋅	⋅	•	Dot operator

Miscellaneous Technical Symbols

Decimal	Entity	Symbol	Description
⌈	⌈	⌈	Left ceiling
⌉	⌉	⌉	Right ceiling
⌊	⌊	⌊	Left floor
⌋	&rfloor	⌋	Right floor
〈	⟨	⟨	Left-pointing angle bracket
〉	⟩	⟩	Right-pointing angle bracket

Geometric Shapes

Decimal	Entity	Symbol	Description
◊	◊	◊	Lozenge

Miscellaneous Symbols

Decimal	Entity	Symbol	Description
♠	♠	♠	Black spade suit
♣	&clubs	♣	Black club suit
♥	♥	♥	Black heart suit
♦	&diams	♦	Black diamond suit

Specifying Color

Because color is presentational, it should be specified with Cascading Style Sheets, not in the (X)HTML document. In both (X)HTML and CSS, color values may be provided by numeric values or standardized color names.

RGB Values

The most common and precise way to specify a color is by its numeric RGB (red, green, blue) values. Using an image-editing tool such as Adobe Photoshop, you can determine the RGB values (on a scale from 0 to 255) for a selected color. For example:

Red: 212 Green: 232 Blue: 119

These values must be converted to their hexadecimal (base-16) equivalents in order to be used as attribute values. In this example, the previous decimal values are converted to hexadecimal.

Red: D4 Green: E8 Blue: 77

In (X)HTML, these values are provided in a six-character string, preceded by the # symbol, like so:

    #D4E877

The underlying syntax is this:

    #RRGGBB

where RR stands for the hexadecimal red value, GG stands for the hexadecimal green value, and BB stands for the hexadecimal blue value.

Fortunately, Adobe Photoshop makes the hexadecimal values for colors readily available at the bottom of the color picker next to the # symbol. The hex values can be copied from the color picker and pasted into a stylesheet or HTML document.

If you are using an image tool that does not list hexadecimal values, you'll need to convert decimal to hexadecimal yourself using a hexadecimal calculator. Windows users can find a hexadecimal calculator in the "Scientific" view of the Windows standard calculator. Mac users with OS X 10.4 (Tiger) can download the free Hex Calculator Widget at:

www.apple.com/downloads/dashboard/calculate_convert/
hexcalculatorwidget.html

Standard Color Names

Colors may also be identified by predefined color names. The syntax for using color names is extremely straightforward.

```
<body link="navy">
```

HTML 4.01 and XHTML 1.0 include 16 valid color names. They are listed here with their equivalent RGB values:

black	#000000	green	#008000
silver	#C0C0C0	lime	#00FF00
gray	#808080	olive	#808000
white	#FFFFFF	yellow	#FFFF00
maroon	#800000	navy	#000080
red	#FF0000	blue	#0000FF
purple	#800080	teal	#008080
fuchsia	#FF00FF	aqua	#00FFFF

These color names may be used with stylesheets as well. The CSS 2.1 Recommendation adds orange (#FFA500) to this list for a total of 17 supported colors. CSS 3 supports 140 additional standard color names that are widely supported by browsers, but they are not valid for use in (X)HTML documents.

3299137

Made in the USA